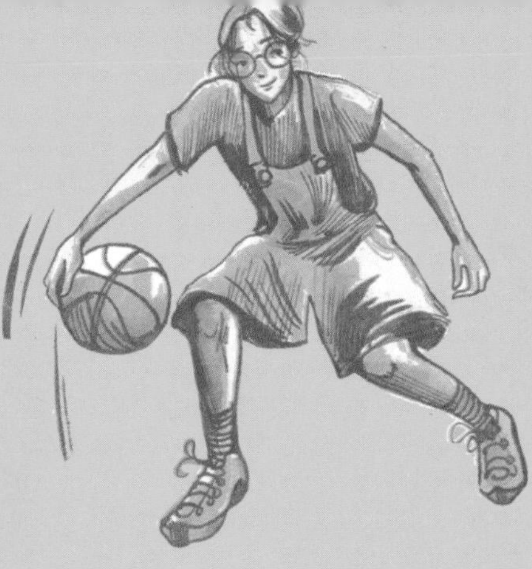

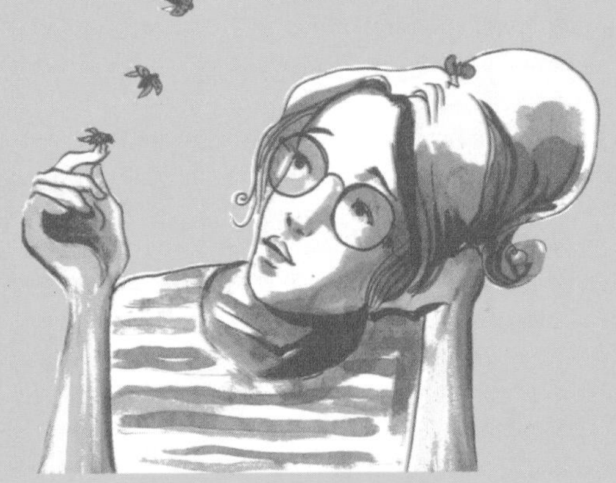

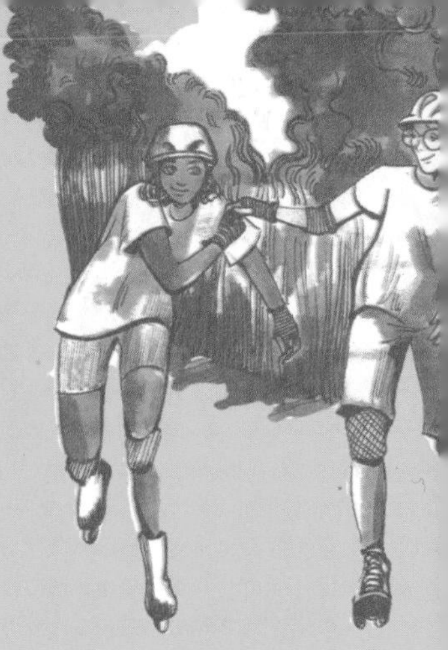

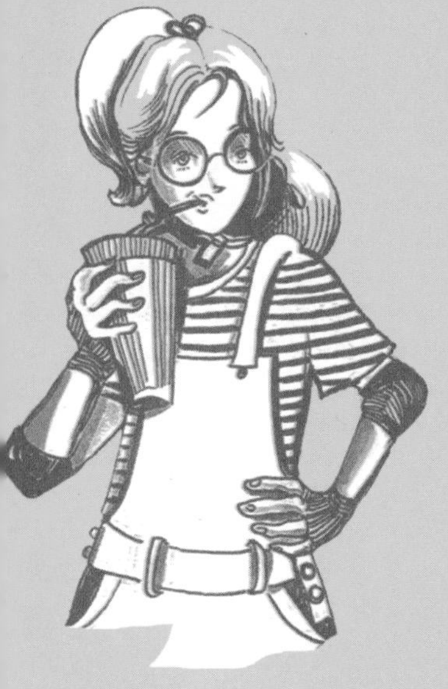

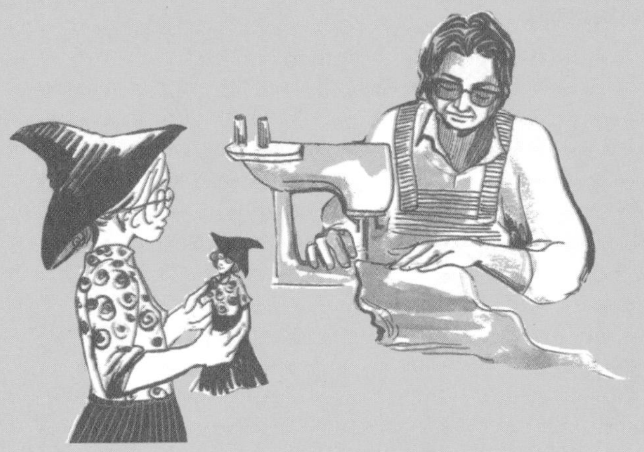

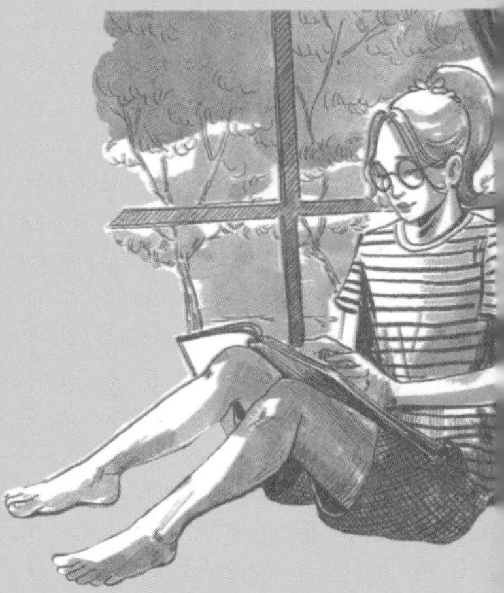

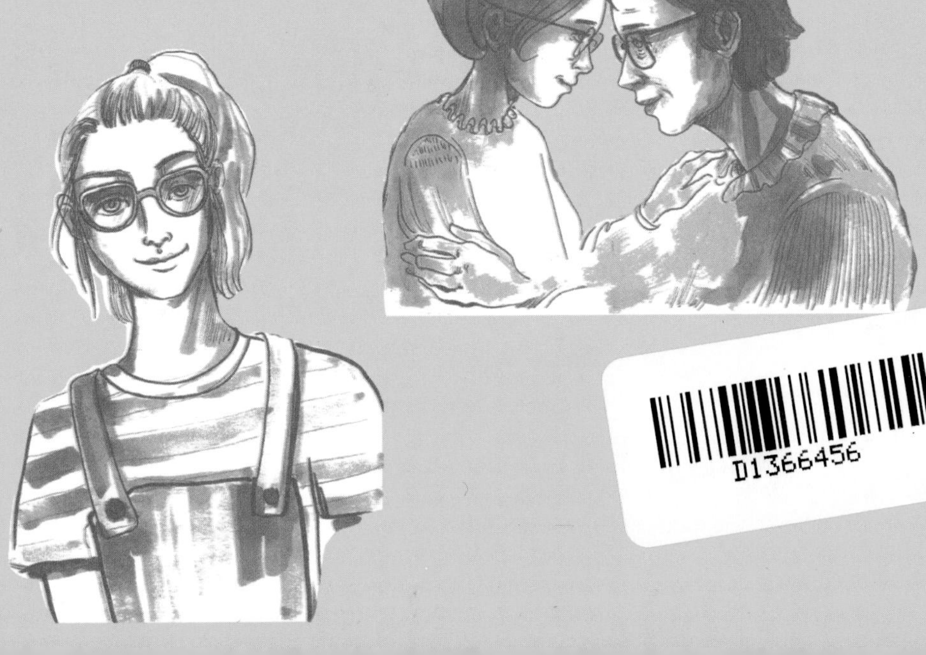

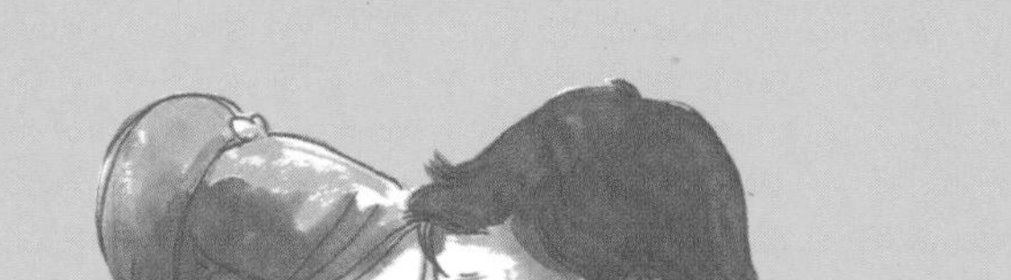

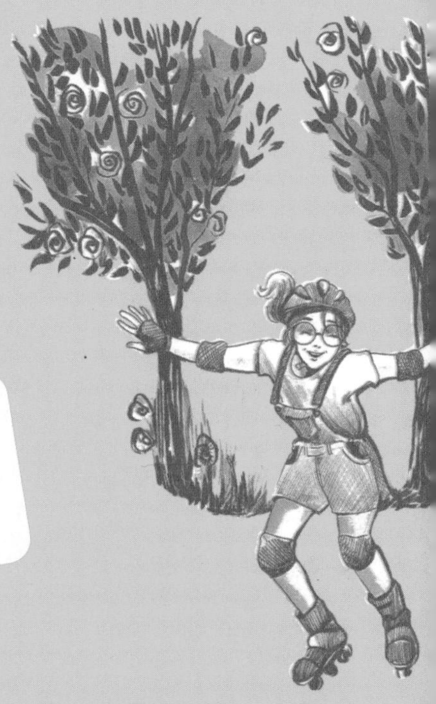

THE COURAGE PARTY

AN AMERICAN SPLENDOR FAMILY / NEURO TWIN BOOK

HELPING OUR RESILIENT CHILDREN UNDERSTAND AND SURVIVE SEXUAL ASSAULT

JOYCE BRABNER
WITH DANIELLE BATONE

ART BY GERTA OPARAKU

MICROCOSM PUBLISHING
PORTLAND, ORE

THE COURAGE PARTY: HELPING OUR RESILIENT CHILDREN UNDERSTAND AND SURVIVE SEXUAL ASSAULT

An American Splendor Family / Neuro Twin Book

© 2018, 2020 Joyce Brabner
written with the help of Danielle Batone
Art by Gerta Oparaku
© This edition Microcosm Publishing 2020
First edition - 3,000 copies - August 25, 2020
ISBN 978-1-62106-785-6
This is Microcosm #355

TO JOIN THE RANKS OF HIGH-CLASS STORES THAT FEATURE MICROCOSM TITLES, TALK TO YOUR LOCAL REP: IN THE U.S. COMO (ATLANTIC), FUJII (MIDWEST), BOOK TRAVELERS WEST (PACIFIC), TURNAROUND IN EUROPE, UTP/MANDA IN CANADA, NEW SOUTH IN AUSTRALIA, AND GPS IN ASIA, AFRICA, INDIA, SOUTH AMERICA, AND OTHER COUNTRIES.

For a catalog, write or visit:
Microcosm Publishing
2752 N Williams Ave.
Portland, OR 97227
www.Microcosm.Pub

If you bought this on Amazon, I'm so sorry because you could have gotten it cheaper and supported a small, independent publisher at www.Microcosm.Pub

You may obtain a free ebook edition from www.CourageParty.com, on Facebook (The Courage Party Book), or by emailing couragepartybook@gmail.com.

LIBRARY OF CONGRESS CATALOGING-IN-PUBLICATION DATA

Names: Brabner, Joyce, author. | Batone, Danielle, author. | Oparaku, Gerta, illustrator.
Title: The courage party / by Joyce Brabner with Danielle Batone ; art by Gerta Oparaku.
Description: [Portland, Oregon] : [Microcosm Publishing], [2018] | Series: American splendor | "An American splendor family comic"--Cover. | Audience: Ages 12+ | Audience: Grades 7-9 | Summary: "Told by Joyce Brabner (American Splendor) about helping her foster daughter Danielle recover from a traumatic experience. This illustrated story for kids and grown-ups is about the 'courage party' thrown for a young girl to celebrate her bravery and ability to work through her feelings and bounce back after being assaulted by a stranger. A valuable resource for teaching children resilience and agency in an uncertain world"-- Provided by publisher.
Identifiers: LCCN 2019037066 (print) | LCCN 2019037067 (ebook) | ISBN 9781621067856 (paperback) | ISBN 9781621065265 (ebook)
Subjects: LCSH: Child sexual abuse--Juvenile literature . | Child sexual abuse--Comic books, strips, etc. | Courage--Juvenile literature. | Courage--Comic books, strips, etc. | Sexually abused girls--Juvenile literature. | Sexually abused girls--Comic books, strips, etc.
Classification: LCC HV6570 .B67 2018 (print) | LCC HV6570 (ebook) | DDC 362.76--dc23
LC record available at https://lccn.loc.gov/2019037066
LC ebook record available at https://lccn.loc.gov/2019037067

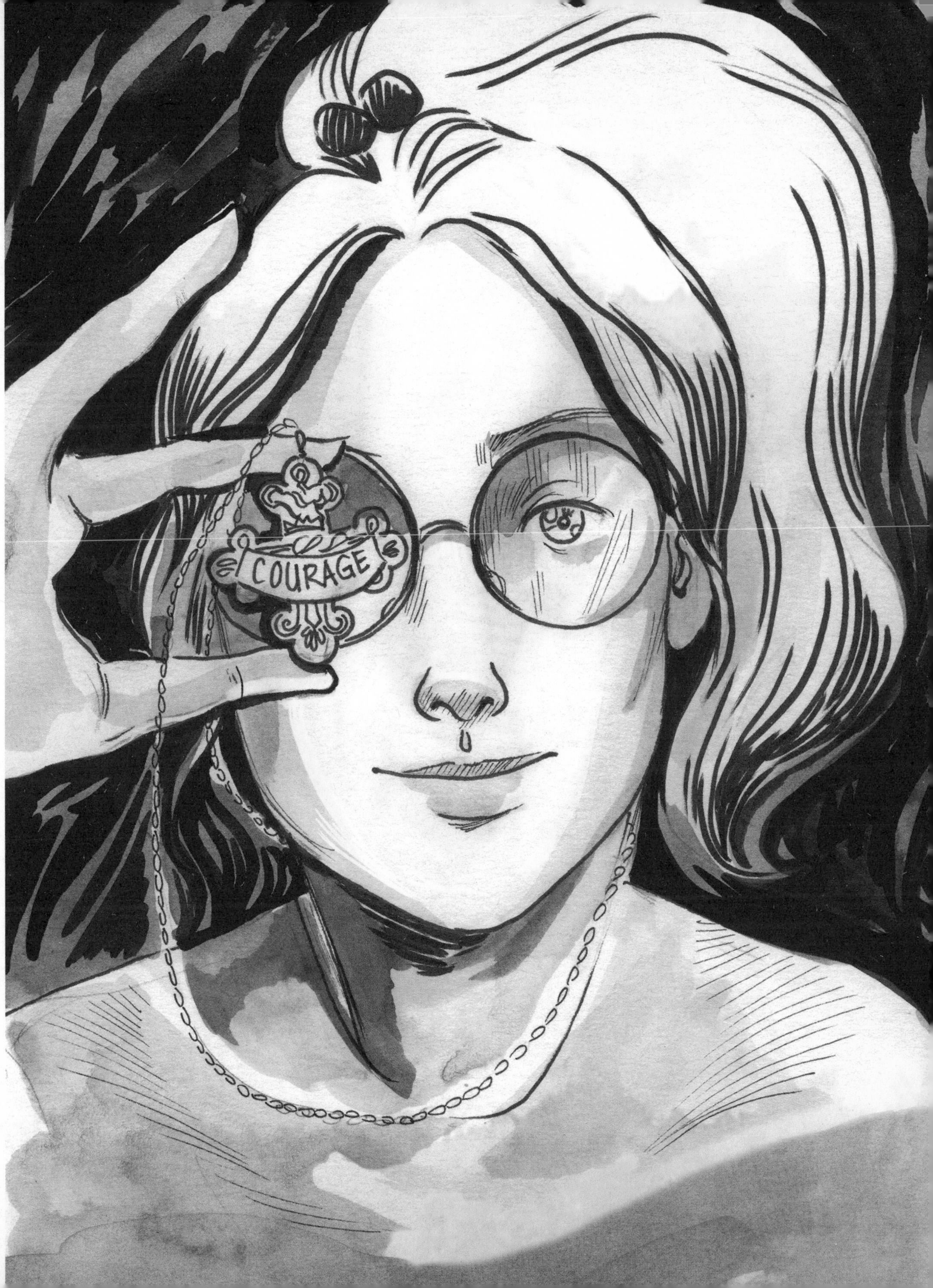
COURAGE

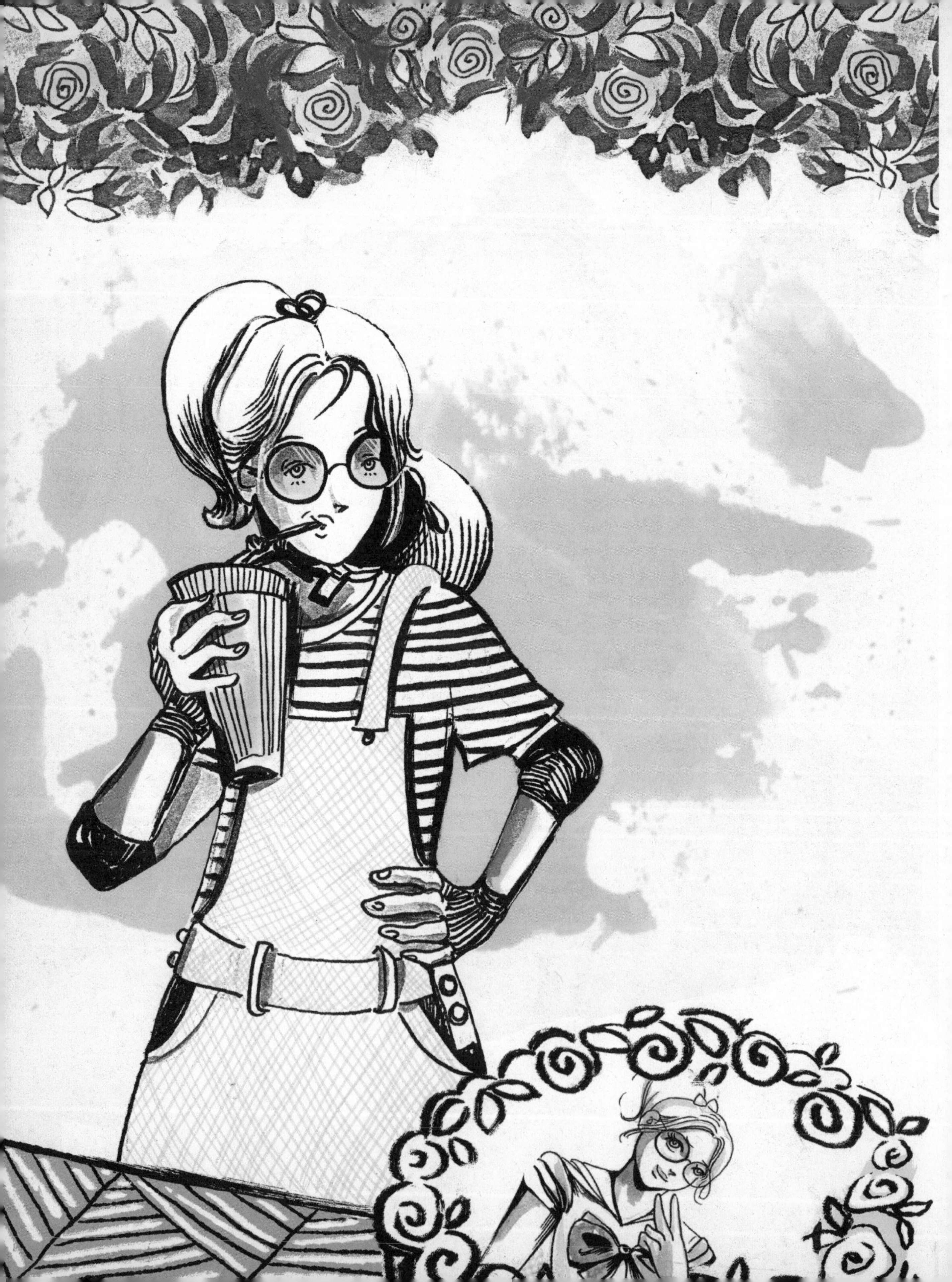

DEDICATION

In memory of Harvey, Rev. Peggy Clason, and Barry (the real Frankie B), all good grownups and child protectors

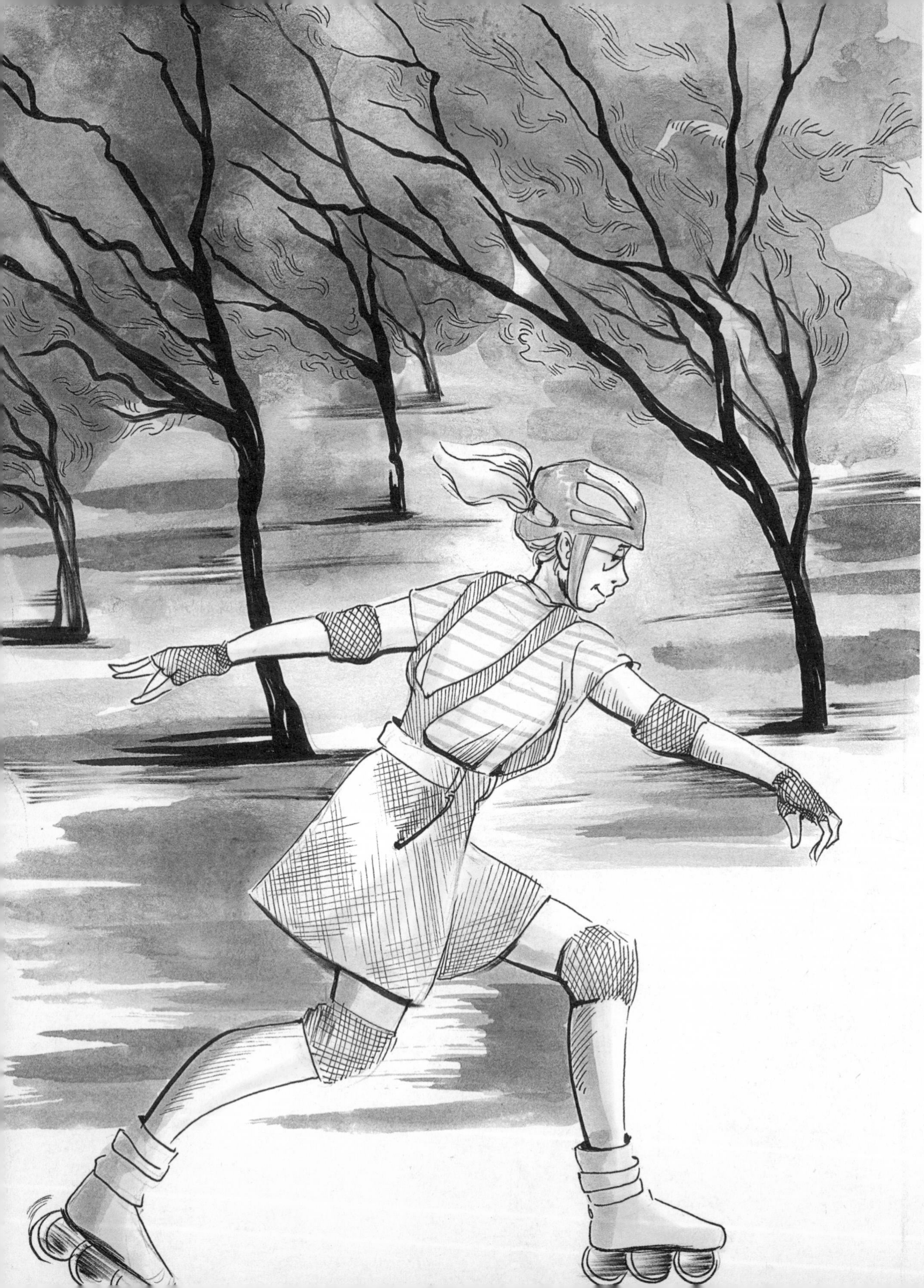

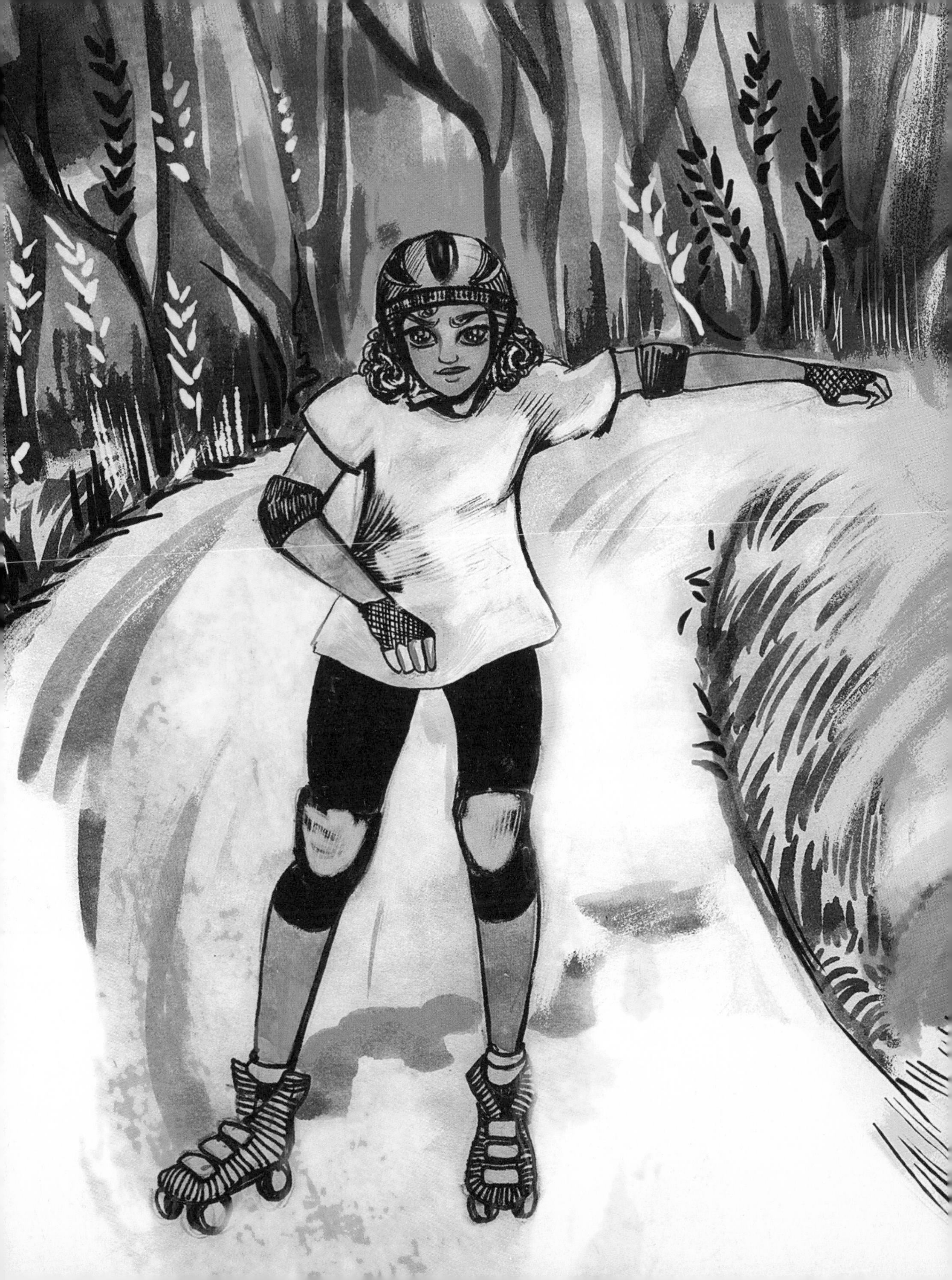

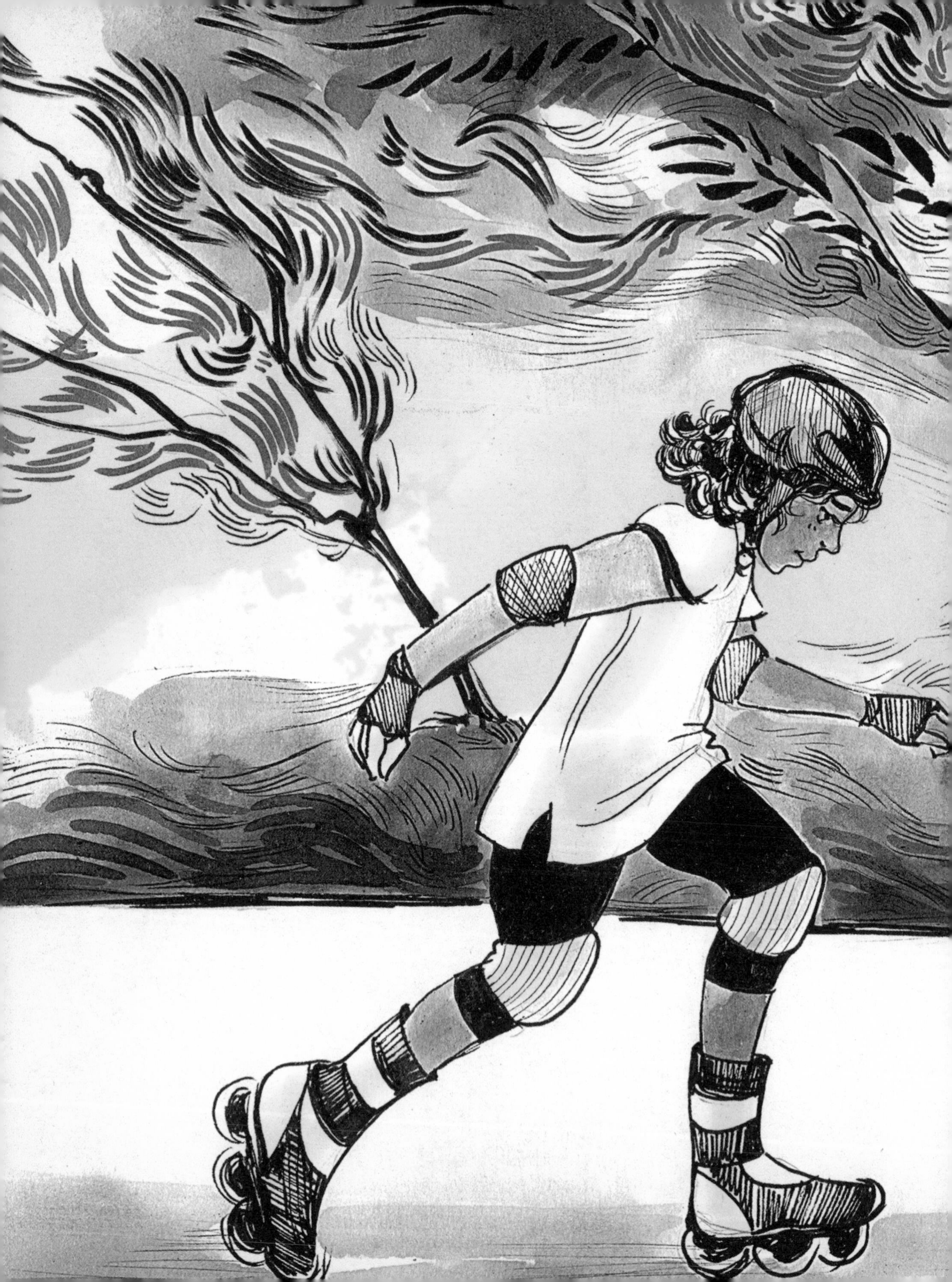

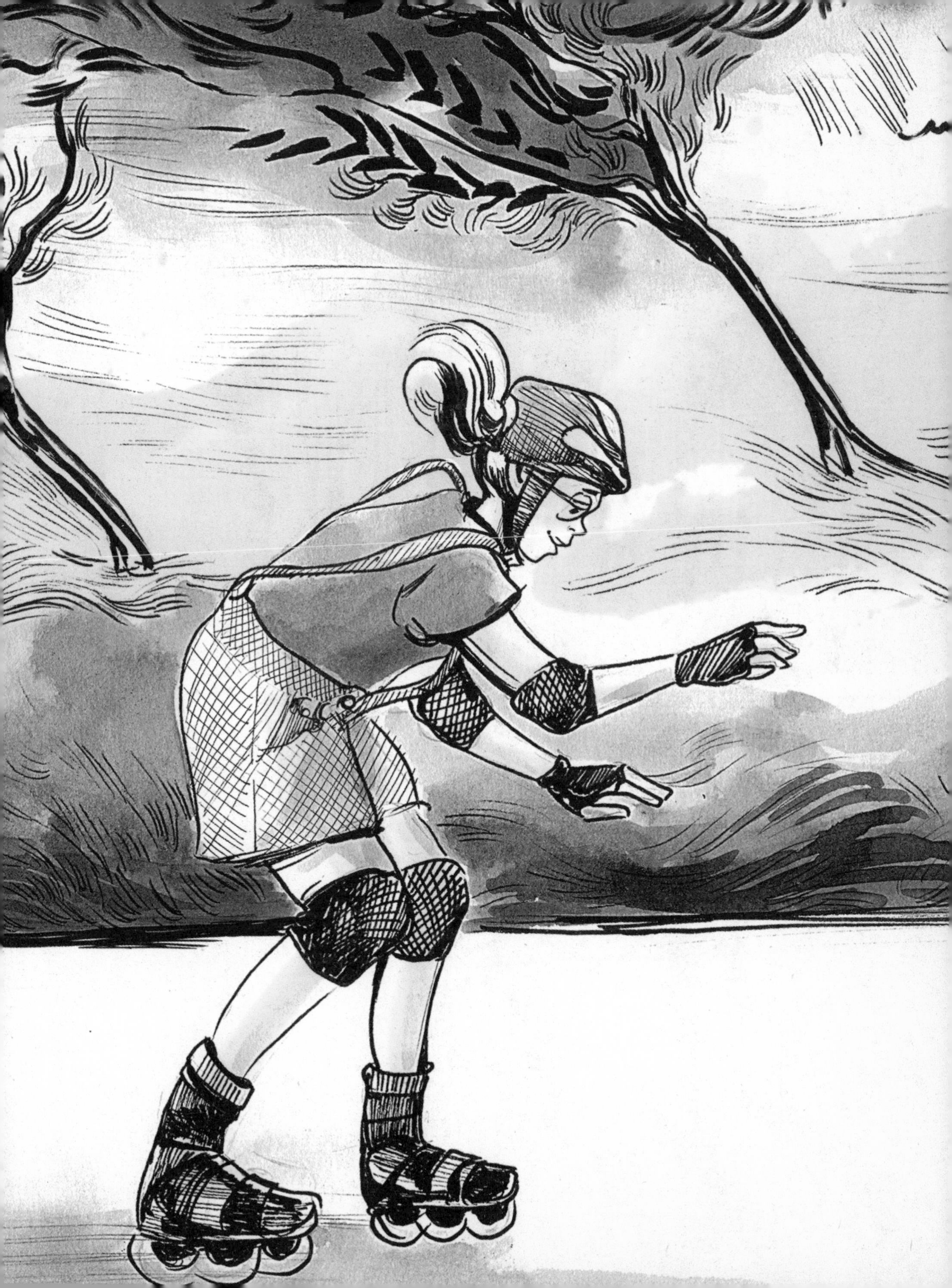

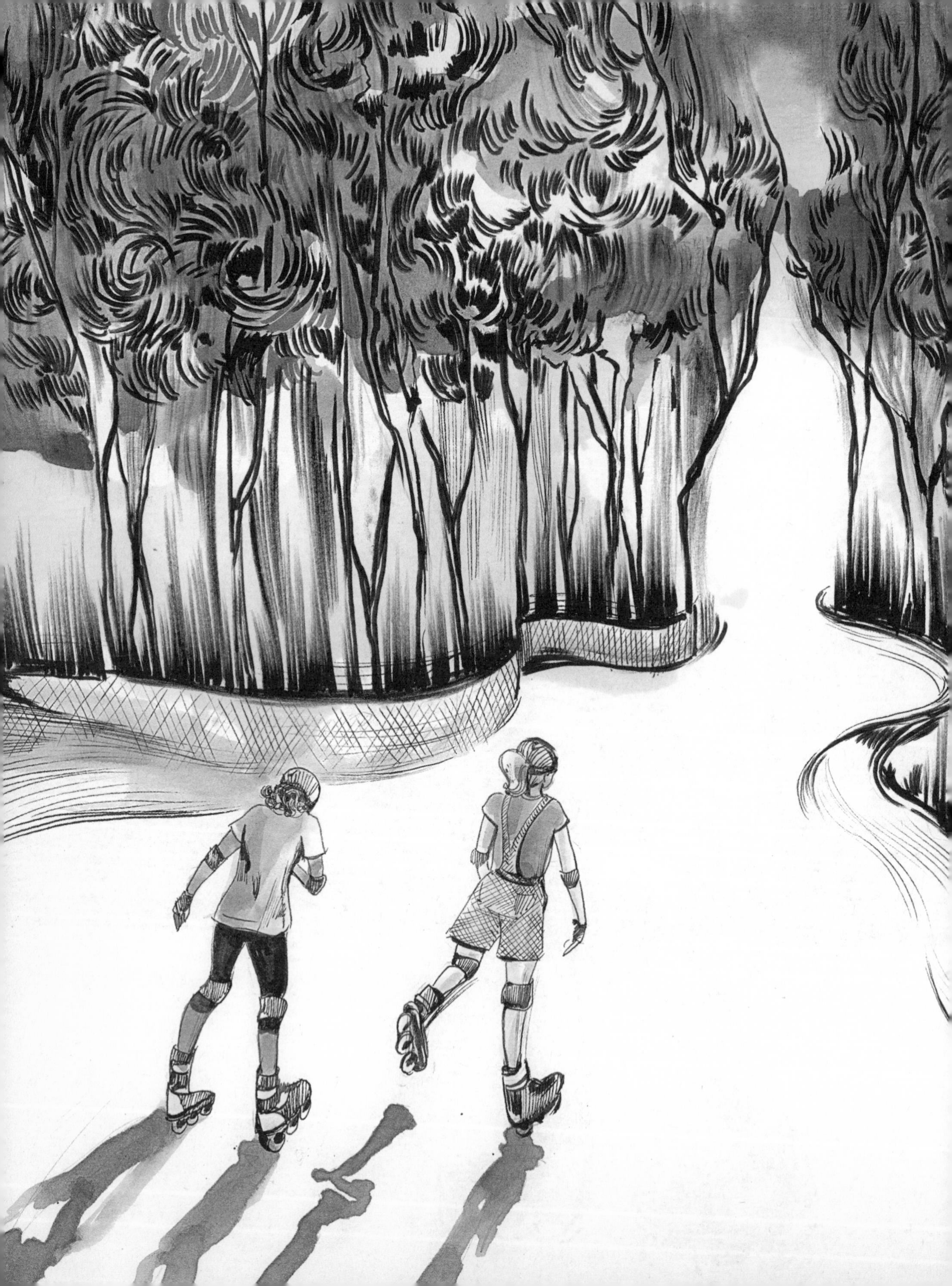

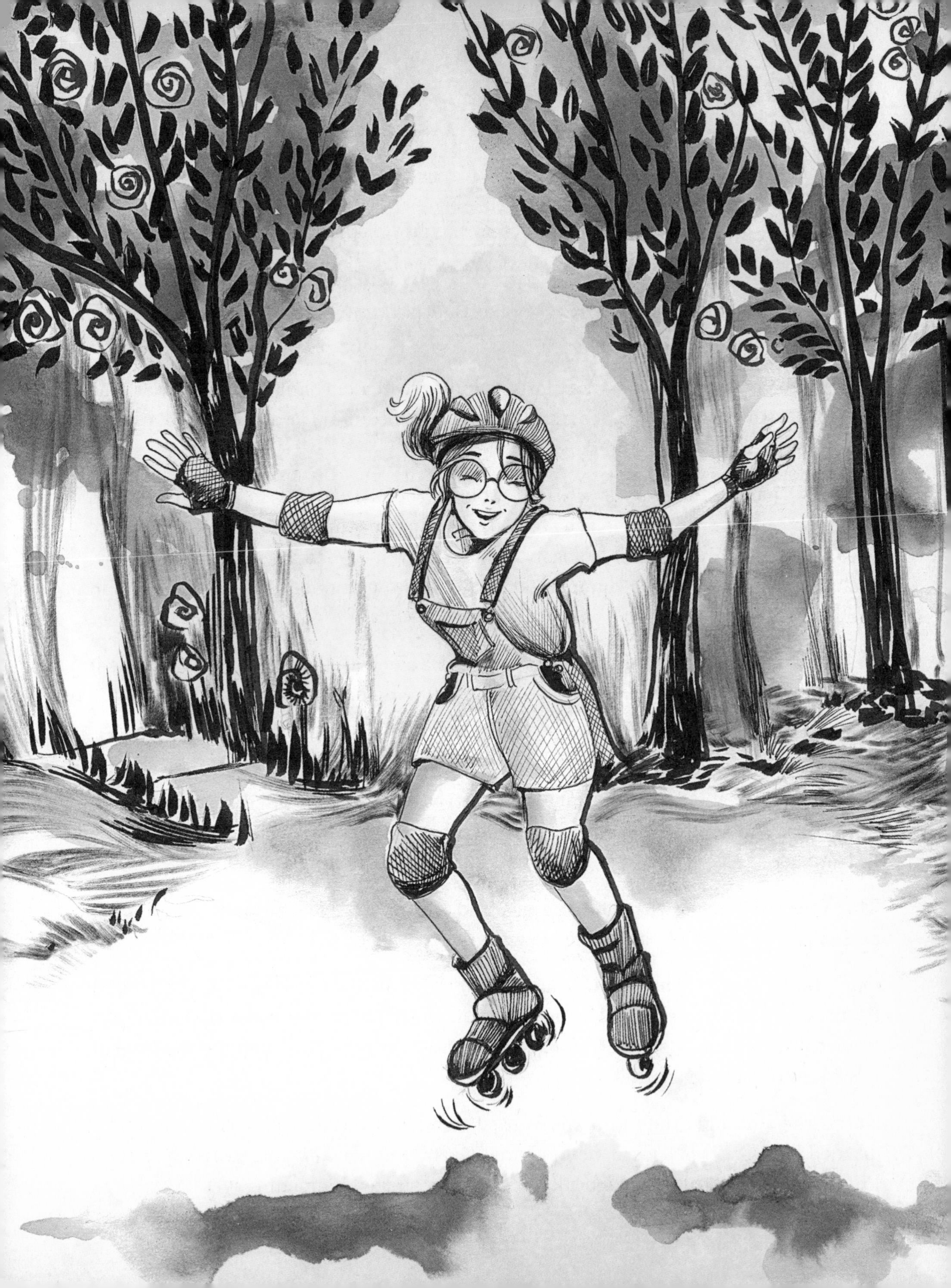

INTRODUCTION

This is a gently explicit book. As a society, we have to move past those times when we kept secrets from our children, especially secrets that leave them vulnerable to harm. Yes, there's some "language" in this book. Yes, there are "situations." But, I think coding such ideas, instead of having the courage to tell our children the truth, is a practice meant to keep adults comfortable rather than to protect kids.

So, if you are a curious kid who just read that paragraph and now may be a little confused, let me put it another way:

This is a book that I think is okay for any kid to read alone, but is much better read together with a parent, a guardian (like I am, in our family) or any other relative or good grownup you know and trust.

The "kid" part of the story is written in black, the pictures are for everybody, and the little pink words outside the story in the margins, are me talking grownup to grownup although I think it is absolutely fine for you to read any word in this book, including all those boring numbers about publishing and dates that you'll find in the front.

I really did organize a Courage Party for our Danielle and I would be very happy if more kids got Courage Parties instead of "conflicting messages," something that is explained later on in this book.

Danielle helped me write this book. She is a grownup now and this story is a combination of what she remembers, what I wrote down in my diary when it all happened, and things I have learned from other people while working to help kids in trouble.

This is a true story, with some names and details changed to make storytelling easier and keep private anything we were asked to keep private.

Our artist lives in Albania, a faraway country that almost no one in the United States can find on the map. Her name is Gerta Oparaku and I met her when she came to the USA to visit me because she wanted to learn how to make the kind of word and picture books that I write.

Gerta and I decided then that we wanted to work together and, after Dani and I decided to make this book, I remembered Gerta and her amazing drawings, stuck in Albania where this kind of book hasn't really started happening, yet.

That makes Gerta a pioneer and the Internet made it possible for us to pass drawings and ideas back and forth, even though we live so very far away from each other. Gerta understood immediately what this book was about and what it was meant to be (As Dr. Anne will tell Danielle at her Courage Party, some things are always the same, no matter how far away you are from home).

GERTA SAYS: Dear kids, it is never too early to build a "support system." Mine since an early age was drawing. I didn't know it would actually help me to grow up and surpass difficulties, I just knew I loved to draw. Creative expression is really helpful ammunition through life. Follow what you love doing and you will discover strength and beauty in every corner of your endless imagination.

JOYCE SAYS: Dear grownups, please listen to our kids. No more conflicting messages. Celebrate our children's honesty and bravery with a Courage Party or your own, even better idea.

Dear Danielle, this is not the first time that someone in your family has told part of your history. There were the stories Harvey wrote and published in *American Splendor* and then, the movie of that same name.

It was not easy getting this book started but, once we did, I think we did it our own way, the way you often explained us to people who asked: as "mother and daughter . . .but without the mother or the daughter." What do you think?

DANIELLE SAYS: Never stop listening to your inner voice. I've known for a long time that my instincts about people have rarely been wrong. You are not a bad person for trusting your gut instincts. Choose to stand up for yourself.

Don't suffer in silence. There will always be someone willing to listen and to help: Keep looking for that one, good grownup you can talk to about things that hurt or bother you.

You can always find one good grownup.

Danielle is now grown up and she has turned into a good, listening kind of grownup. That will happen to you, too, someday. You will be in charge of your life and people will listen. It happened to me, even though I started out scared and worried that no one would ever understand what was happening to me.

My good grownup was a teacher named Mrs. Gail Gardner Kolson, who told me I could grow up and make books. That's why this book is also for teachers like Mrs. Kolson and for Lee, who challenged me with a question I am still answering, and finally, for Stacey who did her job as a counselor with honesty and encouragement and helped untangle some very old, uncomfortable knots.

Joyce Brabner

Cleveland Heights, OH

2018

PART ONE:
HOW I USED MY TRUTH AND COURAGE

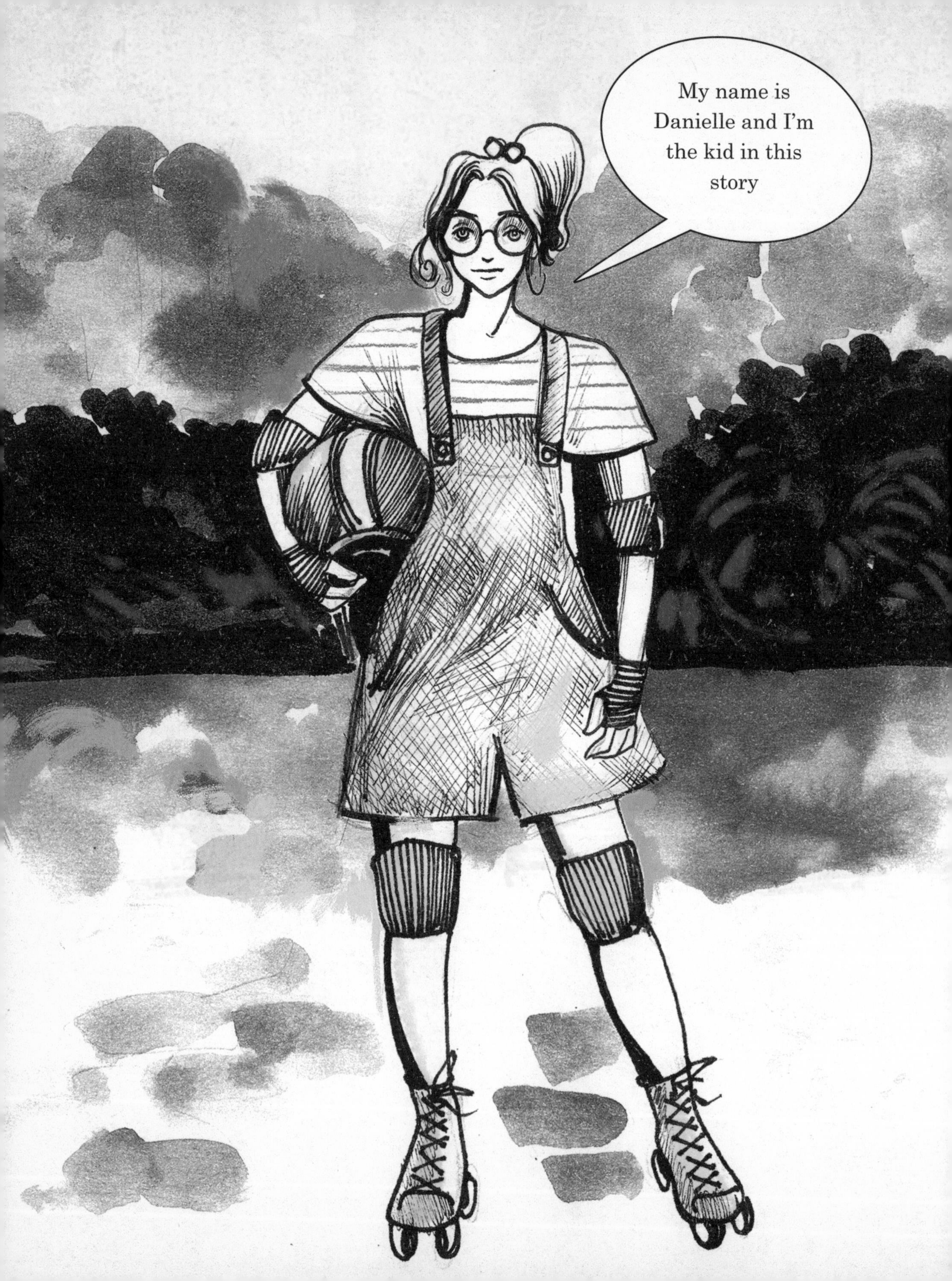
My name is Danielle and I'm the kid in this story

The grownup lady in this story who is like my mother is named Joyce. Sometimes kids in school say, "Joyce is not your real mother!" Then I tell them "I have a mother but I don't live with her. Joyce is my *real* Joyce. She is my guardian and we decided to be a family."

When they ask me why I don't live with my birth mother, I tell them, "That's private. I don't have to tell you all my secrets for us to be friends. Don't ask me any more questions about my private business."

After that, some kids can still be really nosy. They try to push and ask me again and again. Or they tease me.

But what is my private business is my own private business.* What I do next is change the subject. I tell them I am very happy that Joyce is my Joyce and that I am her Danielle.

---

* This is an important idea. Although we talk a lot about being open in this book, our private business is always our private business.

Then I tell them something else that really helps change the subject. I tell them that my Joyce writes comic books about real people and that I am helping her to write one about a real life champion super hero.

That gets them excited and they say, "What do you mean, 'real life'?" "Who is the hero?" "Does the hero wear a cape?" "What are the hero's powers?" and "Is there a bad guy?"

And that's when I really surprise them because I say, "The hero in the story we are writing is me, Danielle, and it is all about something that happened to me when a good guy turned out to really be a bad guy. My secret powers are truth and courage and not only do I have a cape, I have a medal for courage."

Then they say, "I don't believe you. I never saw you wearing any cape!" And I say, "You only see me at school. We have a dress code. Wearing a cape to school is not allowed because it would be distracting."

Then my best friend Keisha says "She is too a hero, because I know the story. Go ahead and show them your courage medal!"

When I do, they start to believe me but they still want to hear the rest of my story. I tell them "I'm tired of talking about this right now. I came out here to shoot hoops. But, I will let you read my story when it is finished."

Do you want to hear my story?

It is a very serious story. There's a real bad guy in the story but you already know that I will get away in the end and be the hero with a medal.

When the bad part of the story was happening to me, I was really scared and no one was there to help me. But later I got away and all the rest of my story is very good.

The bad guy in my story was not an evil super villain. He was an ordinary person, a big boy who tricked me and did a bad thing. He was a criminal.

For a little while, I thought maybe I was bad, too, but my Joyce said, "He is the criminal. And you are a powerful crime fighter." That made me feel better.

Sometimes a movie or a story can seem so real that it scares you. My story really is real and some of it is scary, until the scary part is over and the good stuff starts to happen.

It's okay to read this book by yourself, but it's better if you talk about it or read it with a good grownup.

Not all grownups are good listeners or good helpers. Sometimes you have to look around. You can always find one good grownup, but maybe not right away. If a parent is not a good listener, try a teacher.

If a teacher is not a good listener, try a school counselor. Or a neighbor.

Or someone at your church or temple. Or a friend's parent.

Or your favorite relative.

A good grownup is someone who listens to you when you are scared or upset and then helps you feel better.

My Joyce is one of my good grownups. I also have a favorite teacher and a counselor I can talk to and some grownup lady friends I will tell you about later.

It would be good to read this book with your own best grown up, but if you read it by yourself, remember that . . .

Bad and scary things did happen to me in my story, but in the end I am okay.

Just because something like this happened to me does NOT mean it will happen to you.

Did you notice that there is also some writing on the bottom of this page?* That part is especially written for grownups by Joyce. It's probably not so interesting as my part of the page, which is for kids, but you can read it if you want because in this book there are NO secrets.

* Here it is! Special pink writing!

Things like this can happen to any kid, but we can get help, get safe, and make things better.

If something like this happens to you, it is not your fault. It is something to fix and make better by using the secret powers of truth and courage.

That part of the story comes after the awful scary part, so let's get there as fast as we can.

Hold tight. Be brave with me.

It all started when I went to the park to play basketball. I like to rollerblade and I like to play basketball.

Most of the time, the big boys hog the basketball court, so the rest of us littler kids have to wait . . .

And wait . . .

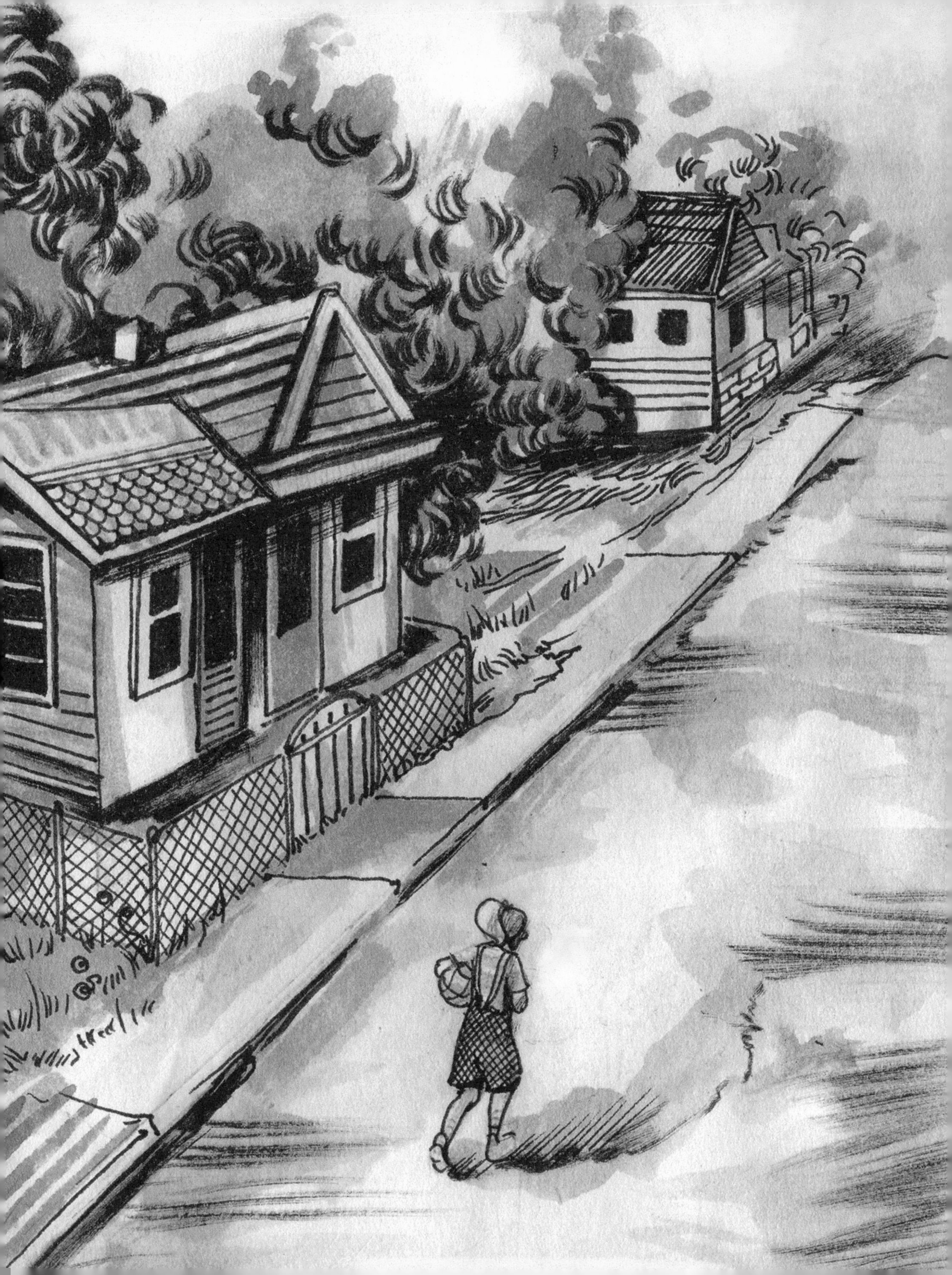

And wait for them to finish up and leave, so we can have our own game.

Even after that, I still had to wait, because I was the only girl that day.

And I'm short.

So, all the boys stuck together and I didn't get picked for the team.

I had to be the substitute, someone who just stands around and watches until one of the other players gets tired or goes home.

I was waiting and watching and feeling very unpopular.

Someone else was watching, too: He was a big kid, who started calling out to the boys what to do, like he was a coach or some kind of basketball champ.

Then he walked out on the court and took one of the little kids' place.*

---

* Does this seem right to you?

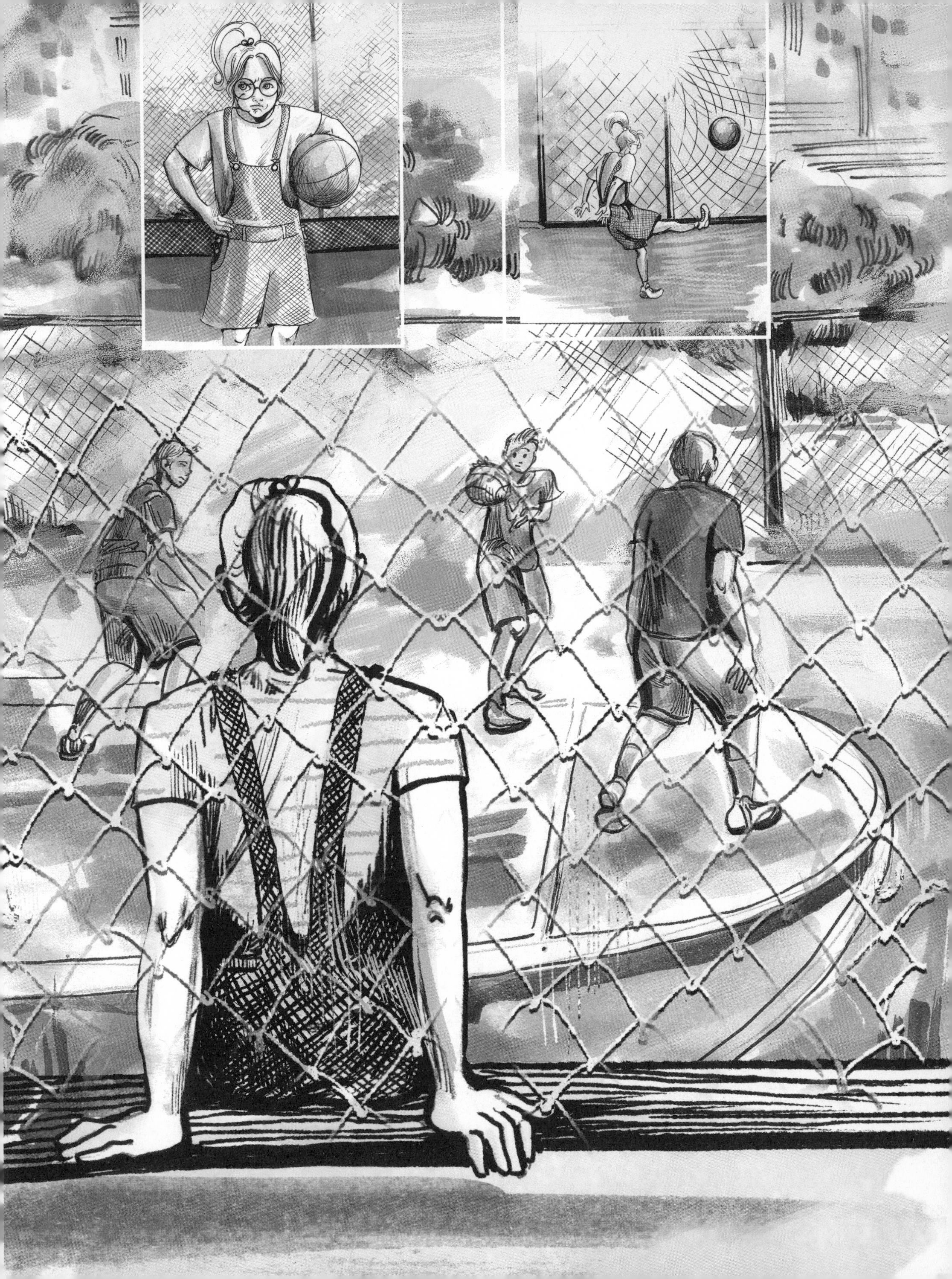

No one complained about the way he was kind of taking over the game, because he was taller than everyone else and able to shoot better and run faster.

No one asked him why he didn't play with the boys his own age or go home with them when their big kid game was over.

No one said, "Hey! It's really Danielle's turn, because she is the substitute who has been waiting in line."

They all liked having a big kid give them attention.

They laughed at his jokes and they cheered when he made points and they all slapped each other on the backs.

I was still waiting and watching and still feeling very unpopular. Until he noticed me.

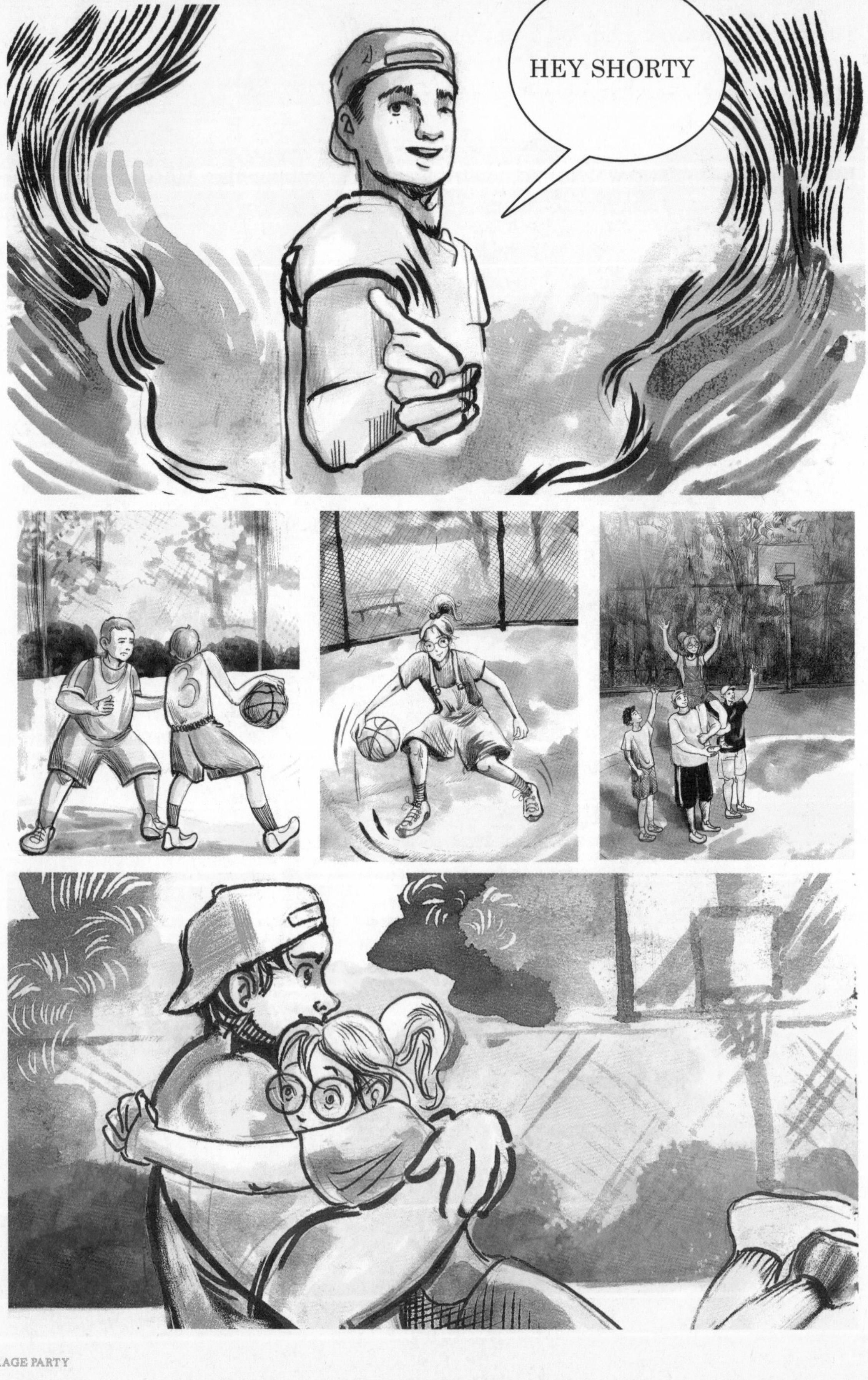
HEY SHORTY

"Hey, Shorty!" he called out to me.

And, when that happened, it felt like the sun just came out.

He made the other boys give me a place on the team. I was determined to show them all that I was just as good. I dribbled, I shot, I scored!

When that happened, the big boy clapped me on the back and had the rest of them pick me up and carry me around on their shoulders, like I just won the whole game.

We played some more. Every time I did something right, the big boy cheered and made a big deal about how good I was. I felt really special and proud of myself.

When I made another basket, he picked me up in a hug and swung me around in a circle. Now it was like we were the only ones playing in the game. He gave me more attention than anyone else. It was like he didn't care anymore about the other boys on the team. Only me.

I don't think the other kids really liked that, but he was big and he had made himself sort of in charge of our whole game. And I guess everyone kind of admired him. Or maybe they were scared to say anything because he was big.

We played some more and the whole game was pretty exciting. Then the big kid made a wild shot. He had the ball and he threw it hard and far but this time it didn't go anywhere near the basket.

The ball went right up over the basket, right on over the fence and way up high until it went down, out into the bushes and trees at the other edge of the park. Wow! Was our ball lost?

The big boy had a funny smile on his face. He said, "Ooops! My bad!" and everybody laughed. "Don't worry," he said.

Then he looked straight at me, with another kind of strange but funny smile on his face, and said to everybody "Me and Shorty will go after it."

He pulled some money out of his pocket and told the next biggest kid to take everybody to the Quick Mart to get soda pops while they waited for us to find our ball.

He said "Take a break and everybody drink up on me. Get some chips if you want. And wait until you're all done to buy mine. I like my colas ice cold!"

So, I ran ahead to the woods. I'm a good finder. I knew I could find the ball right away and I did! It was in way deep and dark, and the branches were scratchy, but I found it and got it out.

He was right behind me. "I knew you could find it! I knew right away, as soon as I saw you, that you were a special girl." He was making me feel all hot and embarrassed. That felt a little bit nice . . . but a little bit uncomfortable.[*]

Then he asked me, "Do you want to see the special place where only the big kids go? It's okay for me to take you, because you are my special girl."

* It's important to learn to listen to your own body. "Uncomfortable" feelings may be warning you that there's danger. How does danger make YOU feel?

That sounded exciting! He said I was his special girl. Maybe that meant that he was my boyfriend. I never had a boyfriend before but some of the popular girls at school talked about boyfriends all the time, so maybe that meant I could be popular with them, too. I said yes.

He pushed away the branches and he showed me a secret path to the secret place. Right away, I knew it was a big kids place. There were some logs you could sit down on and just dirt in the middle, where it looked like somebody had a fire once.

There were candy wrappers on the ground but also lots of cigarette butts and old beer cans and bottles. It was kind of disgusting. I could tell a lot of people had come there before and not cared about using a trash can.

The big boy told me to sit down on one of the logs.

I did not know what was going on. Was he going to propose to me, like in a movie?

He got all quiet for a minute and then he asked me a very strange question.

He said, "What do you like best to put in your mouth?"

I was very surprised, but I told him the truth. I said I liked candy and dessert, of course, and soda pop and chips. Maybe this was where the big kids had picnics when they went out on dates.

When the kids brought his stuff back from the Quick Mart, maybe here was going to be our date.

He smiled and said to me that now we were going to have some real fun.

Now I was going to make him very happy, because I was his special girl. He told me to shut my eyes very tight and not open them at all until he said so.

I closed my eyes tight. Was he going to kiss me? Was he going to make me his girlfriend?

First, I heard I some funny sounds, like he was breathing really fast or . . .You know. Making in-the-bathroom noises, "Unh . . . unh . . ."

And then, just when he said "Okay, now open your mouth and open your eyes!" he grabbed my ponytail really tight, so it hurt.

I opened my eyes and it was awful. He had his shorts and underpants down around his ankles and now his face looked red and mean. All his naked parts were right there in front of my face, ugly and disgusting.

He was not my boyfriend. He was someone who had tricked me. I was frightened.

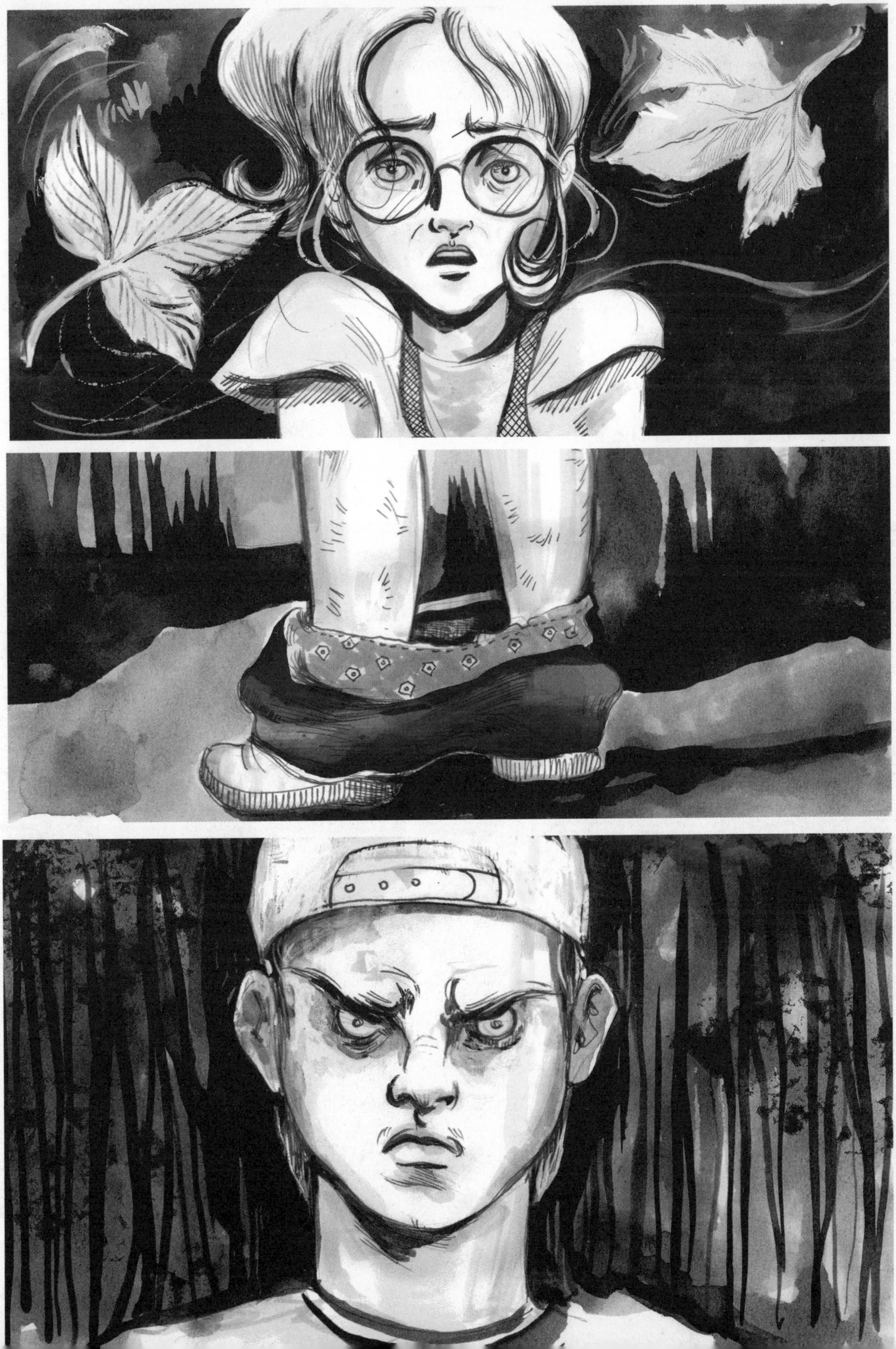

But, I was also very mad. There was a news program that Joyce made me watch with her about "child abduction" and we talked about what to do if a stranger tried to get me to go with them or do something. "Never, ever be afraid to yell and make a lot of noise," she said.[*]

"Being scolded for being noisy, like when you play, is just 'getting in trouble' but being loud to draw attention to yourself if some stranger is trying to get you alone and away from your friends or family is always, always right . . .and you can always say you're sorry later, if your yelling turns out to be a mistake."

He was a stranger.

He got me to go alone with him.

He got me away from the kids I knew.

* If a stranger makes you feel unsafe, what would YOU do?

This is the scariest part of my story, the part I told you would happen. But don't let it frighten you. I want you to know what happened next.

I felt like a fire alarm was going off in my head.

I yelled and I screamed. And I kept yelling and I kicked. I hit with my fists. I scratched with my nails. I bit with my teeth.

He thought I was going to be quiet and just do what he wanted, but I kept moving and fighting and being as loud as I could and he was so surprised by my fighting him back that he let go of my ponytail.

That's when I rolled backwards over the log I was sitting on.

Over and then up, with the log between us.

Up on my knees, crawling, then onto my feet, still really yelling, "Help! Help! Get this guy away from me!"

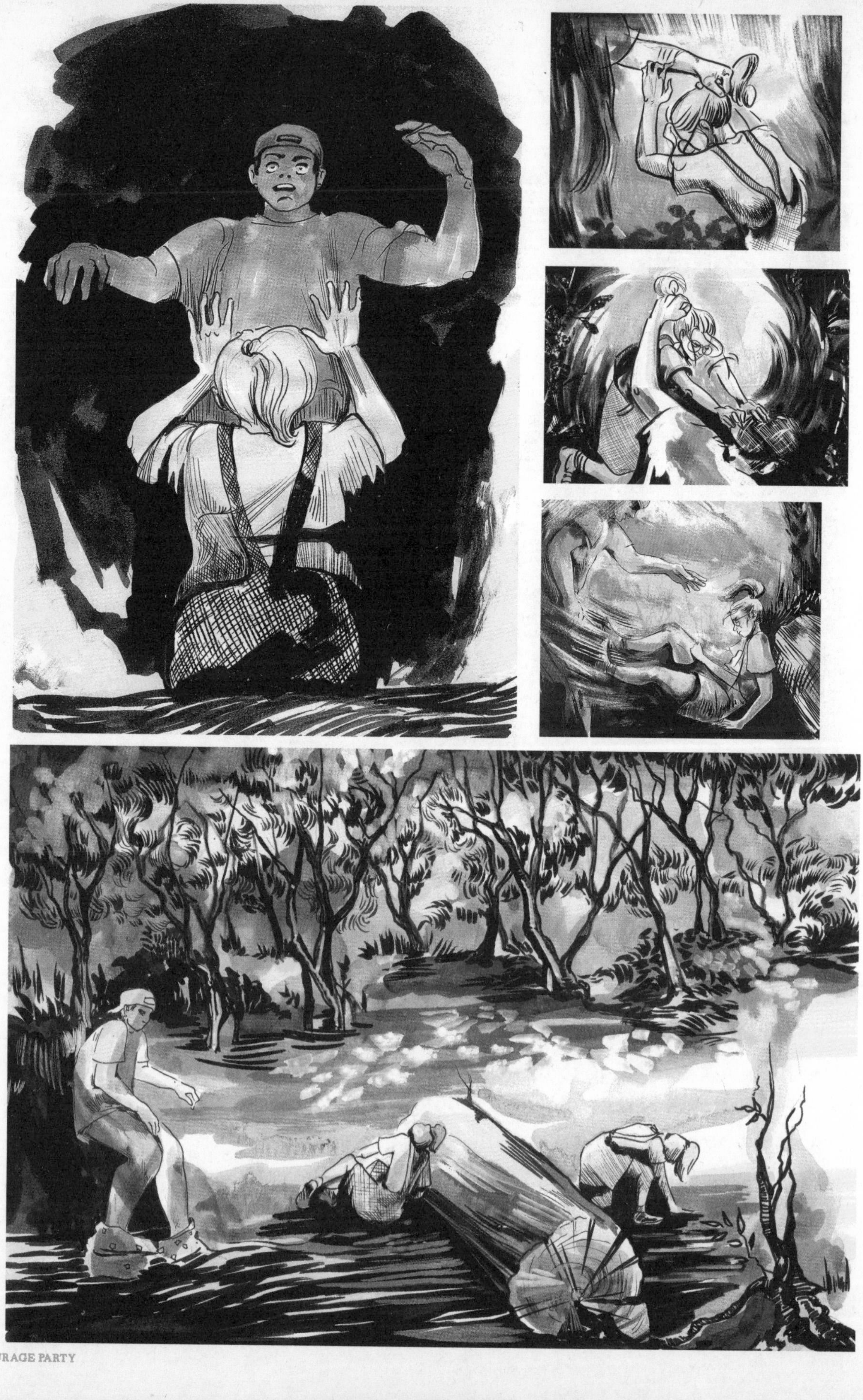

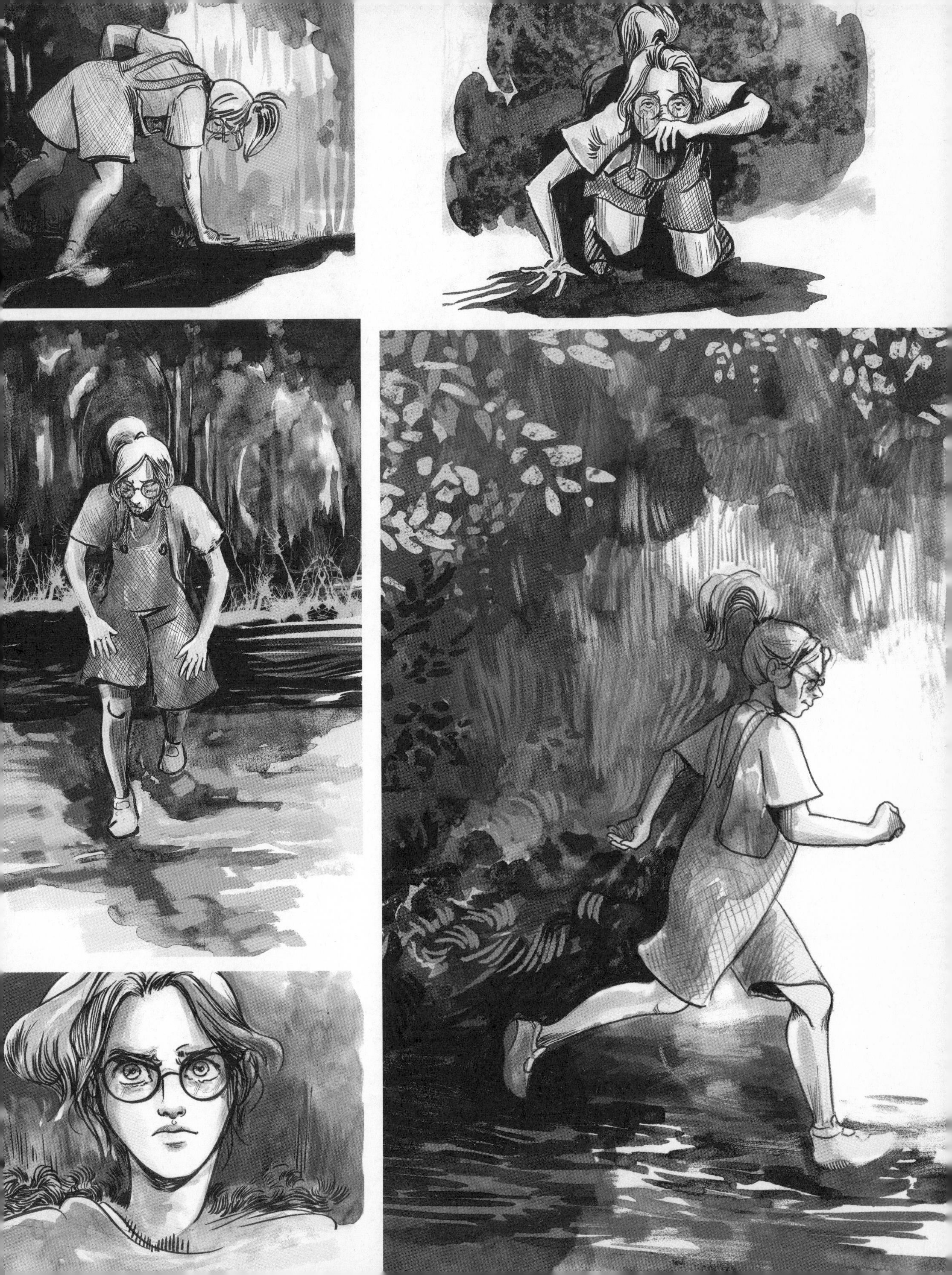

I started to run. I got a head start, because he had to stop to pull his pants up.

I never ran so fast in my life as I followed the path in front of me. Run, run! Yell, yell! Help, Help, help!

All of a sudden, I was out of the bushes, in the part of the park where families have picnics.

There was a mom and dad and some kids staring at me. The dad was getting up and he asked me what was wrong.

Joyce says that if you get in trouble, like an abduction at a shopping mall, you should always run to someone who looks like a mom or any family with kids. That can be a good way to tell who is against abduction.[*]

---

[*] This is a good place to talk about other safety strategies and similar situations. What else could Danielle do?

I think I would have been safe if I stopped with that family. But I was all pumped up with the running and not really sure what was safest for me now and my house was close to the park. So I yelled to the dad, "Keep him away from me! He is a bad guy!"

And I kept running.

I ran the fastest I could run but it seemed the longest way to get home.

Behind me, I could see that the father did stop the big kid. He was talking to him very seriously, like the big kid was in trouble.

I knew the big kid was going to tell lies to get out of it, but I didn't care. I just kept running until I was there at our front steps and then running up them, calling "Joyce, Joyce, Joyce!"

Then there she was, hugging me tight. That ends the scary and dangerous part of my story, so you can take a deep breath like I did after I stopped crying and yelling because now is where I am safe.*

---

* If you're reading this with a good grownup, give each other a hug. Or give yourself a hug!

It was a hot day and Joyce said, "Let's go drink ice water on the porch and think about what we have to do next." She poured me a tall glass and I did something that surprised her and me, something I could have got in trouble for, but didn't.

I was shaking and hot and still breathing hard and I just poured the water all on my head and got soaking wet.

Joyce said that was probably the best thing for me to do and asked if I wanted to take the whole pitcher and do it again. I was not in trouble for that! But, I realized I was now terribly, awfully thirsty and my throat even felt sore from all the yelling and breathing so hard.

We sat on the porch and drank our water, and I told her everything that happened.

Joyce was very quiet and she didn't interrupt me except to ask a few questions at the end. Then, she asked me if I had any big questions for her. I wanted to know more about what the big boy wanted me to do, and she said we would talk more about that, after we took care of business.

When my Joyce says "take care of business" like that, it can mean something hard to do, like cleaning the kitchen floor. Or it can mean someone's in real big trouble.

Was I in trouble? Was I in trouble because I forgot to grab the basketball and give it back to the kids?

"You are in no way at all in any kind of trouble," said Joyce. "This is his fault and only his fault. Not yours.

"You did everything absolutely right and I am so proud of you because what he did was totally wrong, totally illegal, creepy, criminal behavior."

I asked if he was a real criminal, like the guys on some of those TV shows where they all have guns. Or on a picture at the post office.

"I think he's a criminal," said Joyce. "What he did is called 'sexual assault.' We are going to have to report this to the police because he committed a crime against you."

She explained some more words to me that I should know now. I learned what "rape" is and what a "criminal offense" means and what "oral sex" means and what are the adult scientific names for his naked body parts (and mine, too).*

"Some grownups feel very awkward or embarrassed when they talk about sex and bathroom business. Like the way your teacher wants you to say, 'I have to use the restroom,' instead of saying, 'I have to go make a big poop.'

"We're going to use dictionary words when we talk about this with other grownups, so no one gets embarrassed and so we all understand exactly what happened."

---

* In the back of this book is a list of the words Joyce explained to Danielle. See how many YOU know.

I said this was a lot to understand and very confusing and did I really have tell anybody about what happened because it was over now and it really was kind of nasty and embarrassing.

"That is what criminals want you to do," said Joyce. "They want you to feel embarrassed and scared, so they can get away with it and do awful things like this again."

I said okay. I would talk to the police if I could bring my favorite stuffed bear, Blueberry Bear, with me. But I didn't want anyone else to know, because it all was sort of my fault. I let him trick me into going with him into the bushes.

"No way," said Joyce, "No way at all is this your fault. And we are going to talk about it to people because you were brave and you survived all this by yelling and thinking fast and fighting back and telling me the truth about what happened."

Joyce made me turn my face to look straight at her, eye to eye. She took a deep breath and said,

"When people talk to you about this, they are going to use special words you need to know:

Some people will call you a plaintiff. Or witness for the State. Those are lawyer words.

Other people will call you a "survivor" or a "victim." Those words mean they feel sorry about what happened to you. Those words are good enough words, but . . .

Maybe it's because I am a writer, but I always try to use the absolute right word with just the right meaning when I write stories. I think I know the best words for what happened to you.

Someone committed a crime against you. Just like if they came up and grabbed your purse and ran away with it. Purse stealing is called "theft" or "larceny."

The crime he did to you is called 'sexual assault.'

You fought back.

You are a crime fighter. Your secret powers are courage and truth telling.

Police are crime fighters. Wonder Woman is a crime fighter. You are a super crime fighter, too. And a hero. If anybody asks you what happened, you say "I was sexually assaulted at the park. I'm okay now. He committed a crime and I fought back. I'm a crime fighter."

"Who do I tell about this?" I asked.

"Anybody!" said Joyce. "You tell and tell and tell as much as you want. When something like this happens to a kid, they should always tell, no matter what the criminal says to them.

If the person they tell first doesn't believe them, then they have to go find a good grownup who will believe them and help.*

* If something like this happened to you, who would you tell first? And who could you tell second?

If the criminal says they will hurt you or your family or your friends if you tell, you absolutely still tell, because criminals can't be trusted. If anyone talks about hurting your family or friends then good grownups have to be told.

A lying criminal might try to hurt your folks anyway. So it's better for everyone to know right away, to be protected and prepared."

This was a lot to think about, and my head and my stomach still didn't feel right. But Joyce said, "Hold on to Blueberry Bear. I called the police and here comes a police car with someone to talk to us."

Then a policeman walked up the sidewalk to our house. "Hello," he said. "I'm looking for Danielle. I hear you had some problems up at the park. What happened?"

I closed my eyes tight and then I told him, exactly the way Joyce said: "I was sexually assaulted at the park. I'm okay now. He committed a crime and I fought back. I'm a crime fighter."

The policeman made a whistling sound, through his teeth. He said, "Well, then we have a lot in common because I'm a crime fighter, too. I was sent here to help you. I think you may be a very brave young lady.

"I have a daughter your age. I want to hear all about it, he said. I'm here to listen, first. Then we three can decide what to do."

I closed my eyes tighter. I really did not want to tell the whole story again.

"I see you like bears," he said. "And yours is especially blue and handsome. I have a bear, too. He helps me with my listening. Would you like to see him?"

I did. And he went back to his car and brought out a teddy bear that was dressed like a policeman! He had on a little uniform and a badge, a hat, a nightstick, and a belt with a big buckle. "This is my partner, Officer Bruin," said the policeman.

"Does he have a gun?" I asked.

"No. No gun. This is a listening bear. But he has a very important pen clipped inside his pocket that you can use later."

He put Officer Bruin on the steps with me and then he sat down next to me. He had a clipboard and a pen just like the pen Officer Bruin had. He asked me how to spell my name, when my birthday was, and what our address and phone number was.

He also asked me who Joyce was and then he said, "Tell me all about the park. Did you walk there today or ride your bike? Did you go by yourself or with some friends?"

I told him all about what happened. Talking to him was a lot like talking to Joyce, only he had to ask a lot more questions because he did not know me as well. But every time he had to stop and ask me to explain something more, he was very polite.

I thought Joyce had asked all the questions that could be asked about this, but he had lots of new questions and was very interested in my answers.

He said, "Can you describe the big boy's clothing to me?"

I said, "Do you want me to tell about his underclothing, or his overclothing?"

The policeman sat right up and said "Officer Bruin and I really want to know everything you can tell me about what he looks like under and over and what his clothing looks like, over and under. Can you do that?"

I said that I knew that Officer Bruin was a toy bear and really did not think about asking questions.

"This is true," said the policeman, "But sometimes having a bear helps me do the best job I can when I have so many questions. I want to know all about what this guy looked like and every little detail you can remember about him and his clothing. Please tell me."

I took a deep breath. "The boy was wearing black and white basketball shorts. Black with a white stripe.

"The label inside had just a big red C. But, his underpants were long, like basketball shorts, too. They were bright red, a shiny material with all little diamonds that had tiny holes inside them that were yellow dots to match the yellow stitching on the underpants and the waistband said whole words, 'Diamond Championship.'

"His t-shirt was just plain white and he kept it on. And his sneakers were . . . Is it okay if I draw them? They had fancy designs."

The policeman gave me the Officer Bruin pen and turned over the back of one of his papers. When I was all finished, I showed it to him.

"I know exactly what those sneakers are. And all about his underwear. You are a very observant young lady and a talented artist."

He wrote some more things down on his clipboard and then handed me one of the papers. "This is where I wrote down what you told me. I would like you and Joyce to read it over.

"If I left anything out or got something wrong, please say so. Otherwise, would you both please sign at the bottom, next to where I put the date?"

We read it carefully. We did not find any mistakes and we took turns signing. He said I should keep the pen because it had his phone number and I could call him any time, from now on.

I said, "You are a good listener and a very talented writer."

That made everybody laugh. But, the next thing he said was very serious and made me get all cold inside. He said,

"Now I'd like you both to get in the car with me. Let's see if we can find this guy and ask him a few questions. My policeman partner is already at the park, talking to a family that saw something."

I was really scared. I did not want to see the big kid ever again. Joyce held my hand and said, "Time to take care of business." But my feet did not want to move.

The policeman noticed and said, "I'm going to ask Joyce to sit inside next to me first. Take a look at the windows on my car. You can see out but . . ."

The windows had dark stuff on them. When they were rolled up, it was very hard for anyone to see inside. The policeman said, "You can sit on Joyce's lap. Blueberry Bear can sit on yours. We can see out. Nobody can see in and I'll be right beside you."

I got inside. We drove up to the park. At the end of the street I thought we were all going to have to get out and walk to the basketball court but, instead, the policeman did something amazing!

He drove right up on the grass and kept going through the park. There was another police car already there and some of the kids I knew from the game.

Our policeman seemed to know everybody's names. He said, "Stay inside the car while I go talk to my partner. Do you know that boy, Michael, from school?"

I said yes, I did. He was in my class last year. He asked me if Michael was one of the boys who played in that game with me and the big kid. I told him, no. But Michael had watched us play, because he was waiting for his friends to come with their skateboards.

I saw the policeman talk to Michael and some other kids. Then his partner pointed up the hill and two of the other kids pointed up there, too, and they talked some more about something.

The partner policeman got in his car and started to drive through the rest of the park and up the hill. Then our policeman got in his car and said we had to follow. He thought he knew the big kid's name now and where he lived.

I did not want to see him. The policeman seemed to know I was thinking that, and said all I had to do was stay in the car and talk to him about anything I saw.

The first thing I saw was a lady I did not know standing in front of a house talking loudly to the partner policeman. Then she started to yell. She was really angry.

"My boy is a good boy!" she yelled. The policeman talked to her some more and then, all of a sudden, there he was! The big kid. Only now he was wearing a red tracksuit and another kind of sneakers.

"Is that the guy?" asked our policeman.

I said yes, I could tell from his face. But his clothes were different. Did that mean no one would believe me now and his family would think I was just causing him trouble?

"Stay here," said our policeman. He got out of the car. His mother was still yelling, but now the other policeman was asking the big boy questions.

Our policeman went up and talked to everybody. He looked at the big boy and pointed down at his shoe and the boy bent down and tied a loose shoelace.

Then everybody talked some more, his mother started yelling even louder, and the boy got in the back seat of the one policeman's car, and our policeman came back and got in our car.

Joyce had a big question all over her face. "Did he . . .?"

Our policeman gave a big smile and said, "He didn't change those red diamond and yellow stitched satin undershorts! I was able to see them when he bent down to tie that shoe!"

"Good crime fighting, Danielle! You gave us a good clue!" said everybody.

"Is it over now?" I asked. I wanted to go home and I was worried about the yelling lady and what Michael would say at school.

"Not yet," said Joyce. We will have more business to take care of later but we also have to get some dinner and then . . ."

"Oh no!" I didn't think I could take any more crime fighting business.

Joyce hugged me tight. We were home and ready to get out of the police car. She whispered to me on top of my head, "You are a terrific kid. I'll have a surprise for you later."

The policeman shook my hand before he left and gave us each a white card with names and phone numbers. He told me these were names of people who would call Joyce soon, to decide when we could have a meeting.

He said, "Sometimes when there is a sexual assault, we give people a ride to see their doctor. Let me ask you one more time. Think carefully. Did he do anything that hurt you anywhere on your body, especially in between your legs or in your bottom or mouth or anywhere else that you forgot to tell me or Joyce?"

I told him he pulled my ponytail hard, but not enough to pull any hair out. There were places where I had bruises on my arms and legs that came from fighting. I had tree scratches. But nothing hurt me between my legs or in my butt or in my mouth.

He took a long look at me and then he said, "I believe everything you told me. And you were very lucky. This boy did something wrong but you did everything you could to protect yourself. I'm proud to know you.

"I'm going to tell my daughter and other little kids your story, but I won't tell anyone your real name or where this happened. That's a policeman rule, to keep everything private."

Then he said goodbye.

I asked Joyce if the keep-my-name-private thing was because what happened was so bad that I was supposed to be ashamed. Joyce said no, it was something called a "policy" which means a rule, like the rule "no hats on in the building" we have in school.

We were just about to go inside, when Mrs. Kent, our nicest neighbor from across the street came running over.

"Is everything okay? I saw the police car. Is anyone hurt?"

Joyce said, "We had a little trouble this afternoon. Danielle can explain. It's her story."

I said, "I was sexually assaulted at the park. I'm okay now. A big boy committed a crime and I fought back. I'm a crime fighter."

Mrs. Kent had a kind of surprised look on her face at first. Then she reached out and gave me a very big hug. She said

"I'm very sorry this happened to you. Are you really okay?"

I said, "Well, at first I was very scared. Then I poured a glass of cold water on my head, to cool down because I ran so fast. The policeman was a good listener. And now I'm hungry. My stomach has stopped hurting."

Mrs. Kent said, "I'm glad you are feeling better. And I am very glad you told me what happened. Something like this happened to me when I was a little girl and everyone told me not to say a word to anyone about it because it was an awful shame."

I said, "Do you mean 'ashamed of you'?"

Mrs. Kent said, "It felt like that. As if I was the bad one, instead of the person who hurt me. So I felt bad, like I had to keep a bad secret. And I didn't tell anyone except my mother until I was a grownup. After that I felt better because when something like this happens, you should tell and tell and tell. No secrets!"

I asked her, "Does Mr. Kent know what happened to you?"

Mrs. Kent said, "Yes he does. I married a wonderful and kind man who is very understanding. And my little sister knows everything and so does my best girlfriend. So I feel okay. Not scared or ashamed."

Joyce said, "Mrs. Kent and I both have good men in our lives. But sexual assault is something that women understand especially well because it happens more to us than to boys. It *does* happen to boys and men. People can forget that.

"Now it's time for me to tell you about a special woman thing that is one of the things that will be happening to you, soon. Besides talking to the person on the white card, there is going to be a party for you."

I didn't understand what she meant. I already had my birthday. The next party I was going to have was supposed to be the day before I started back to school and got my new backpack and school supplies. But that wouldn't be until the end of summer, when the outdoor swimming pool closed down.

Joyce said, "We are going to have a Courage Party for you, to celebrate your bravery. I'm going to invite our best grownup women friends to come and listen to you tell your story. Then each woman will tell you her own story and there will be a special cake that you will design for Cory the baker at Zagara's to make. And presents. Surprises.

"You can plan the menu and have all your favorite foods. Mrs. Kent, will you come to our Courage Party?"

Mrs. Kent said, "Of course I will. What a wonderful idea. I wish someone had given me a Courage Party. It would have helped me feel much better about myself."

I said I was sorry she didn't have a party but that she could share mine. Mrs. Kent laughed and asked me what food should she bring.

I said, "Could we have some of Mr. Kent's famous barbecue ribs, like he made for the block party?"

Mrs. Kent said she was sure Mr. Kent would be happy to cook barbecue ribs for such a brave girl.

Then she asked Joyce if it would be okay to tell him what the Courage Party was for and what she should say if anyone else asked about the police car in front of our house or anything.

Joyce said, "The person you should ask is Danielle. It's her story."

I said, "Just say I went to the park to play basketball. A boy I didn't know threw the ball into the bushes, to trick me into going with him alone. He assaulted me but I fought back real hard and got away and ran.

"We called the police. They took him away because what he did was a crime. It was scary, but I'm okay now. I'm a crime fighter and soon I'm going to have a ladies' Courage Party, so thank you for the barbecue ribs. They are the best I ever tasted."

Mrs. Kent smiled and gave me another hug. Then everybody went home because it was dinnertime. Joyce said I could have my favorite anything, even breakfast. So, we had waffles and eggs and orange juice and after dinner Joyce had us sit down with some drawing paper, colored markers and her red notebook.

"Time to plan your party. First show me some design ideas for a Courage Cake for the bravest girl in the house. And tell me what you want to drink, because we will serve drinks. Anything you want!"

I asked Joyce, "Does it have to be a good-for-me drink, or can it be a good-to-taste drink?"

Joyce wrinkled up her nose and said, "Your choice. For this party, the vitamins do not have to be invited."

I thought about some bottles I saw at the grocery store. There were some that had pretty green soda. And next to them were blue ones. I told Joyce.

"Lime soda pop. And blueberry, I think. A six pack of each and maybe some iced tea for our guests, too.

"Who are our guests going to be?" I asked. "I know we're having Mrs. Kent."

"I have a list of our friends who I think would really understand what a Courage Party is all about," said Joyce. "Here's who I would choose:

- Reverend Peggy, because she is so wise and understanding

- Kaffers, because she is your and my best adult woman friend

- Dr. Anne, because we like her and I know she has done a lot of traveling all around the world and has a lot of stories

- Mrs. Kent and you and me, okay?*

I liked everyone Joyce chose, so she started to make the calls while I drew designs for the cake. She called Kaffers, who asked to talk to me so I could tell her I was all right. Kaffers said she was coming and would make baked beans.

Then came Dr. Anne, who would be working but said she would take the afternoon off and to tell me she was proud of me for being gutsy and a tough cookie and she would make a salad.

She told me I should come in and see her the next morning and Joyce said, "Absolutely right. Of course."

---

* Who would you invite to your own Courage Party?

Then Joyce said she was going to call Reverend Peggy and ask her if we could have the Courage Party in her little Meeting Room, the one with the big round table and the flowers.

Joyce took the phone into the next room but I listened in. It was funny. I heard Joyce explain everything to Reverend Peggy, who would bake bread.

I heard Joyce say, "Danielle respects you because you are old, so she might try to be too polite and not talk openly about what happened. So, it will be important that she hears you say the P word—penis.

"Then she can relax and talk freely about what happened. We use correct names for everything." Then Peggy said something and Joyce said "This all sounds good" and they both said goodbye.

I asked Joyce if "correct names" meant dictionary words. Joyce said yes and that Reverend Peggy was a dictionary word person only sometimes, like when she was doing her job and giving a service.

I said I understood and that now I had some cake designs to show Cory who can make frosting pictures on cakes, like an artist, at the bakery. I wanted chocolate inside and blue roses all around, like a picture that I drew.

For the cake picture, I drew my favorite Japanese cartoon super powered girl. Her sisters all have special abilities, ginormous big round eyes and long, rainbow-colored hair.

I picked the one who was the shortest (like me) but also the fastest, who could get out of traps because she little enough to wiggle out or squeeze between or climb through a mouse hole. She was an escape artist and so was I!

The super girl had a very bad temper because sometimes they tried to make her stay behind because she was little. Her face would turn pink and little lines would appear to show how mad she was about that, but she always got to go anyway, even if she had to sneak out.

However, when there was a fight, she was always the best fighter. Her face would go first pink and then red. Little lines around her would go all buzzy like an angry bee or lightning.

Also, the super girl had a special pink cape that she wore when she was on a mission. Otherwise she and all the other super girls wore sailor shirts and skirts and went to school unless they got the signal to go do something important.

Joyce said Cory would be able to do a good job and that this would be an interesting cake. She told me that it might be better if we went on a Joyce and Danielle adventure tomorrow instead of me going to the park.

I said I didn't think I ever wanted to go back there again and Joyce said she understood and I could take my time.

"We will go see Dr. Anne first," said Joyce. "She will want to hear more about what happened and she'll look you over before she writes a report for our policeman."

Joyce told me that after that, we would go to the dinosaur museum and the aquarium. She said that boy could not keep me from enjoying myself playing basketball so, the next time I wanted to play, she would come to the park and watch. But I was sick of basketball for now.

The next morning, Joyce took me to see Dr. Anne. She gave me a big hug and told me, "I'm so sorry this happened to you. I'm here to make sure you are all right. Do you want Joyce or a nurse to stay in here with you, while I check you out?"

I said no, because I have been going to see Dr. Anne by myself for a long time. Joyce nodded and I went in to the room that has her exam table/couch thing and all the charts on the wall.

"Today we are going to give you a special kind of examination," said Dr. Anne. "Before I ask you to undress, we are going to make a special drawing." Dr. Anne took a big roll of brown paper out from behind her table and started to roll it onto the floor.

I like to draw, but this seemed very strange to me. Dr. Anne smiled.

"We are going to make a big picture of you. Lie down on the paper and I will draw an outline of your entire body with this marker, all around you. Then I will ask you to sit on the floor with me and fill in all the details."

We did that. The picture of me looked like a great big shadow and I asked Dr. Anne if we could cut it out so it would be like Peter Pan's shadow.

"What a wonderful idea!" said Dr. Anne. "We'll do that first. Then you can color everything in."

I drew my eyes, nose and mouth first. Then my hair. I asked Dr. Anne what kind of clothes should I put on myself.

"No clothes, yet" said Dr. Anne. "First, we have to get to the bottom of all this."

I nodded, but I was not sure what she meant. Dr. Anne explained some more.

"You are smart enough to know that a doctor's office is not exactly an art room," she said. "But I have markers and crayons here so you can draw what I need to see to understand what happened to you.

"I want you to think very carefully and then draw or show me everything you can remember that boy did to you, where you were touched, where you were hurt—the entire story.

"It's very important for you to show me the whole picture so, take your time and while you are drawing I am going to get us some juice boxes and cookies. My son baked oatmeal raisin cookies for his school bake sale last night and they were so good that I bought half of them to take to work and share with everyone!"

The cookies were very good. I ate mine while I drew everything I could remember, where I got scraped, bruised, kicked, and grabbed.

"He pulled my ponytail hard," I said. "That's on the back of my head. Should I turn my shadow picture over and show where?"

Dr. Anne nodded. Then she said, "While we are looking at that side of you, my lovely lady, let's draw anything else that happened to you on your back or here, where your butt is. Did he touch you or hurt you there, on your bottom?"

I shook my head hard. No way! I was too fast for him and, besides, I kicked and scratched.

"Let's turn you over," said Dr. Anne. "What about here, on the other side?"

She pointed to the place between my legs. "Did he touch you here with his fingers, with his penis or anything else?"

I knew at once that it was time to use scientific dictionary words, like Joyce said, because Dr. Anne was asking me about "penis."

I told her, "No. He did not touch my vagina with his fingers, his penis or anything else. But, he showed me his penis and tried to make me do something with it and that was disgusting and scary."

Dr. Anne nodded. "I'll bet it was. I'm very glad to know that you are okay now. Do you have any questions you want to ask me?"

I was not sure. There was something that was bothering me, so I thought for a minute and then I said, "I think I have two questions. Can I ask them both?"

"Of course!" said Dr. Anne. "Doctors like it when their patients ask questions because we are usually interested in knowing about the same things. What is question #1?"

I said, "You know about sexual intercourse, right? How the man puts his penis in the woman's vagina so they can have a baby?"

Dr. Anne smiled. "I believe I know something about that. I am a doctor but I also had a baby myself, and it all started with a penis and a vagina."

I said, "I was pretty sure that's how you did it, with the sperms and the egg. Unless your son was adopted."

Dr. Anne said, "No. We did it the old fashioned way. We had sexual intercourse. My baby son grew inside me and when the time was right, he squeezed out through my vagina.

"He was very little then but it was still a tight fit. I had to open up wide and push hard from inside. When he finally arrived, we wiped him off and gave him his name."

"Was the part where your husband used his penis to have sex with you awful and disgusting, like what happened to me with that boy?

"Did it, did it . . . hurt?" I asked that because someday I might want to have a baby, too, and I needed to know.

"Good questions!" said Dr. Anne. "When two people want to have sexual intercourse together, it is really very nice. It is an adult kind of fun that happens with love and closeness.

"It often feels like tickling each other and rolling around playing, and hugging and kissing, and other good feelings that happen inside grownup bodies, whose special body parts are developed."

"Like growing breasts?" I asked.

"Exactly," said Dr. Anne. "But you don't start having sexual intercourse just because you have breasts, or hair between your legs and under your arms. You have to think it all over first and decide for yourself when you are ready.

"When you start to grow breasts and pubic hair I will be happy to talk to you about how and when you can decide about that."

"The hair part sounds icky and scratchy," I said.

"It's all part of the package, my dear. But talking about that is for another time, for later. Right now, you have a super streamlined kid body that is designed for you to do kid things. Things you like to do.

"And you had another question for me."

I was still thinking about the hair. The boy who hurt me had hair down there and I wanted to know . . .

"Was he trying to make a baby with me? Was he trying to have roll around fun sex, like with you and your husband? Or movie star sex, like when the woman closes her eyes and they play all the music?"

Dr. Anne thought for a minute. "You ask the best questions, Danielle. People get very confused about sexual assault, because the word 'sex' is part of that idea. But sexual assault is not about making babies or moving your bodies together in an adult, loving way.

"To begin with, sexual assault means one person did not give permission for their body to be used in a sexual way.

"No permission means it's wrong. That's the law for everybody.

"There is also a special law that has to do with children. Children cannot give permission to an adult for their body to be used in a sexual way. Even if they think they are giving permission, they cannot give permission to be sexually touched, to have sexual pictures taken, or to make sex movies.

"I'm not talking about naked mommy and her new baby pictures. Or if your dad helps you change into your swimsuit in the family locker room.

"I'm talking about bad touching and scary looking at your body by big people who use their eyes or cameras, especially cell phone or computer cameras to make sex pictures or videos to put on the Internet. And people who show kids these videos and pictures and call them 'our special secret.'"

All of a sudden, I got very worried. I forgot that I had a secret from long ago. I did not want Dr. Anne to get mad at me, but all this was very confusing and maybe I had done a bad thing without understanding it, when I was little.

I decided to ask her.* Joyce always says, "It is always better to know than to not know" and I knew this next question would stick in my head forever until I knew.

"I think I did a bad thing," I said. "When I was in preschool, this boy named Ethan sneaked in when I was on the potty and after he saw me, I told him he had to show me his, too, or I would tell the teacher. I saw his penis. Was that sexual assault?"

Dr. Anne did not look angry. She said, "That's another wonderful question, Danielle. We're really starting to understand all this.

* If you could ask Dr. Anne any question, what would you ask? Would you like to hear my own grown-up answers about sexual assault and sexual intercourse?

"I think Ethan was just being rude. Or nosy. Bathroom business is supposed to be private, but some little kids don't learn that until after preschool.

"Here's how to know:

"Did either of you use force or hurt each other? Or threaten to use force? Or was this normal little kid curiosity between two normal little kids who were equals because they were the same age?"

I said I thought we were just curious. I know other kids who did the same kind of thing: boys with girls, boys with boys, and girls with girls.

Dr. Anne continued and I was starting to feel better. "Rape and sexual assault are not the same thing as two equal friends giving permission to do sexual things.

"Sexual assault means some kind of threat or force was used and here's the tricky part that a lot of people, even adults, have trouble understanding, so I want you to really listen:

"Sexual assault or rape is not about loving sexual intercourse, no matter what happens with anyone's body parts. Rape and sexual assault are about force or violence and about having power over someone else.

"Do you understand what I mean?"

I was not sure. I could understand the violence part. He hurt me and tried to force me. But I was not sure about the "power over" thing or why he would want to do that to me. So I asked Dr. Anne and she gave me her answer.

"Did you ever see a kid act all big around the little kids and show off? Or boss them around? Or force them to do things they did not want to do?"

I knew what she meant about show-off big kids. Dr. Anne kept going.

"The way I heard it, the boy who hurt you was bigger than all the rest of you kids. And he sort of took over your basketball game.

"Did that seem a little funny to you?"

I remembered thinking something like that, too. He did kind of make himself in charge. And I thought it was funny he didn't play with kids his own age. I told that to Dr. Anne and she said,

"There are big kids who are really nice to little kids for good reasons. My teenage son is part of a mentor club for third graders. He and his friends help them with their homework and then they play games at the rec center until their parents come to pick them up. You could even say that when some big kids help little kids with school and sports that they are helping them grow up to become more powerful.

"Powering up. Power *with*, not power over. Do you understand?

"I think the boy who hurt you in the park might be someone who had something bad, maybe even something like a sexual assault, happen to him. Something that made him feel terrible about himself.

"Whatever it was, now he seems to be the kind of kid who thinks he has to prove he is important and powerful. But instead of hanging with kids his own age, he is out there running the little kids and hurting some of them.

"He was not being loving. He did not have permission. He was trying to have power over you, to make himself feel big, but you did not give him that. You fought back.

"I am pretty sure you are not the first little kid he has sexually assaulted. But I think you are going to be the first one to stand up and say 'No more!'

"That boy crossed a line. He is not just an unhappy kid with a sad story. He is now a criminal who is big enough to hurt kids littler than he is. I think that's what he likes to do."

That made me think. Were there other kids, maybe kids littler than me, who he hurt too? Kids he forced to do things they did not want to do? Kids who could not get away?

And were they all too scared to do anything or say anything?

"I don't like that," I said. "I don't like to think about him hurting me and I don't like to think of him hurting other kids who could not get away, like I did."

Dr. Anne looked at me for a long time. Then she said something that made me feel kind of shivery inside.

"That's why you are different. He may have already hurt other kids and made them his victims. If he is not stopped, he could go on to hurt a lot of other people. But you are the crime fighter who is going to stop him.

"First, give me another hug, my brave, brave girl. And then, hop up onto my funny table here. I am going to have you put each foot in one of these things that are called stirrups so I can get a good look between your legs."

"What are you looking for?"

"Well . . . I usually tell little girls I'm checking their girl parts to make sure they did not turn into a frog or something. But that's a joke I use to help them relax."

I was trying to relax, but it felt very funny to have my legs spread so far apart, like I was trying to do the splits on my back. I wanted to know what was really going on. Not some frog joke, and I told her that.

"You deserve to know the whole story, so here it is: I am checking for once and for all to make sure you did not get hurt in between your legs. First I will look at the outer parts, to see if there are any cuts or bruises.

"I will use this special plastic tool to see inside your vagina. It looks a little like a duck's bill and if you hold it like this, you can make it quack.

"If you like, I can show you with a mirror everything that is happening. I will tell you what I am going to do, every step of the way and any time you say stop, I will.

"It's all a little awkward, I'll admit, but it's very important to be able to report to the police what I've seen today and what you have told me with your drawings. And also, let me show you my new camera.

"When we are done with the in-between-your-legs part and a quick check of your bottom, I am going to take some pictures of the rest of your bruises and scratches from the assault. Those pictures will go in the report, where only special people with permission will look at them."

I showed Dr. Anne the band-aid on my knee, from where I fell rollerblading last Saturday. "This is not something he did to me. It was there already."

Dr. Anne smiled. "This what makes you a great crime fighter and a good kid. You tell the truth. You have the power of truth and courage to fight back against what happened and to help other little kids."

"I'm not so little," I said.

"No, indeed!" said Dr. Anne. "And when we are done with all this funny business, I would like to take a picture of us together that I can put on my desk, in my office."

I said that was okay, so long as I got to change back into my own clothes. She was right about the plastic thing, which is called a speculum (SPECK-you-lum). It does look like a duck's bill and Dr. Anne showed me how to make it "quack." But it's not much fun. You can't really play with it like a toy.

The whole exam was weird and sometimes a little uncomfortable but like we say at home, we were "taking care of business." And Dr. Anne explained things in an interesting way and showed me more stuff and answered all my questions.

I like it when grownups answer my questions instead of saying I'm too young to understand, because a smart grownup can always find a way to explain it so a kid can understand, even just a little.*

I was learning a lot that morning. Still, my feelings were going up and down. I felt shaky and strange and sometimes really mad, even though Dr. Anne was being really nice.

If I was one of those big eye girls in a Japanese cartoon, I bet here is where they would show my head getting bigger and bigger with all the stuff I had to think about.

---

* Children don't need long, detailed answers but they do need to feel confident that you are telling them age-appropriate truth. It always helps to ask other parents or pediatricians how they answer children's questions.

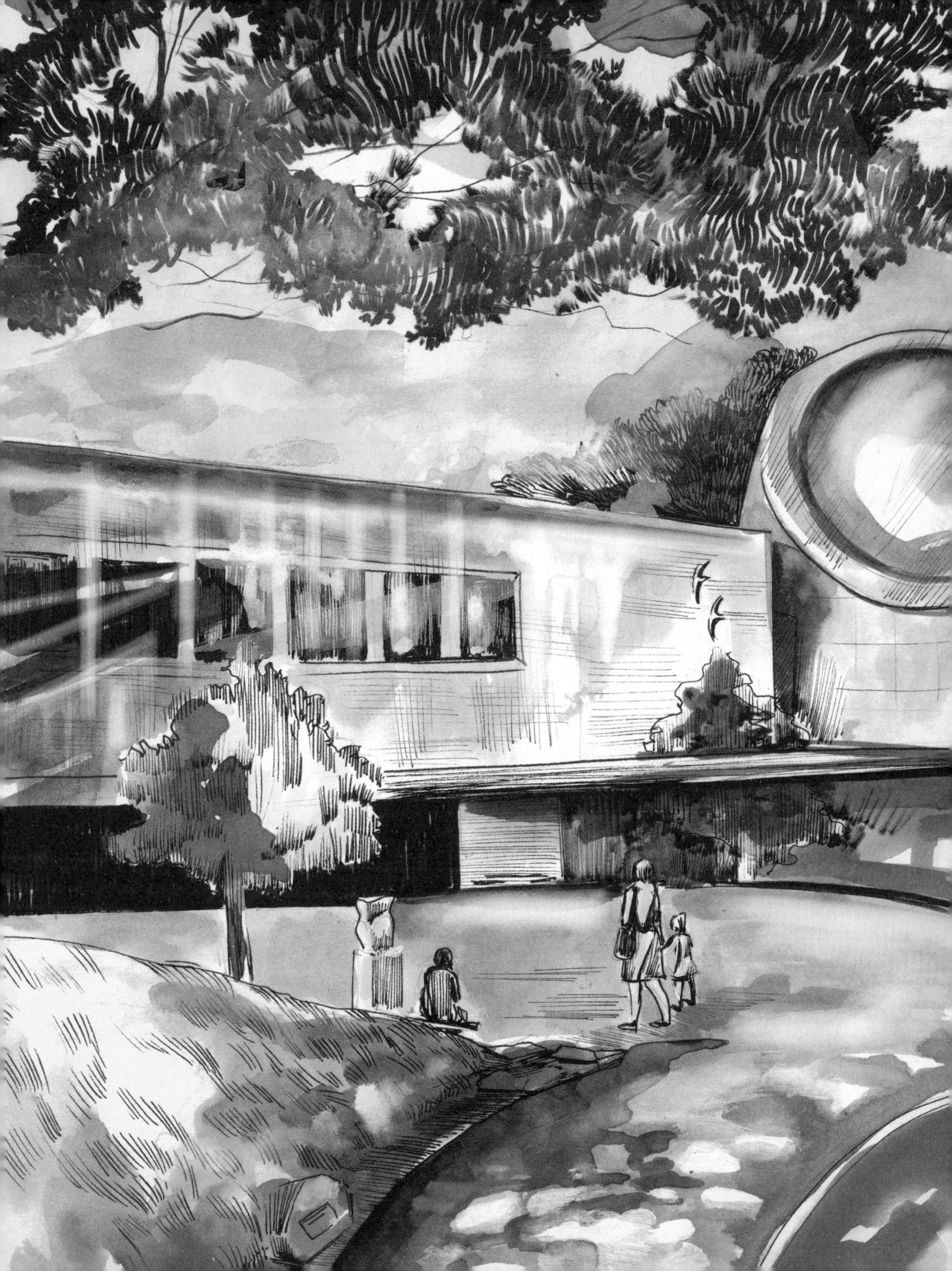

There would be all kinds of wiggly lines and zigzag lines and other stuff flying around me—my head especially. My face would probably change color to angry red, then pale yellow nervous and who knows what else? Maybe green, like one of Dr. Anne's girl frogs.

After I came out of the exam room and we were walking to our car, Joyce asked me if anything hurt when I was in there, or was it just strange and a little uncomfortable?

I told her I learned a lot, but could we please not talk about it now and Joyce said, "Definitely understood! For the rest of today, we will only do things you want to do and try to have a lot of fun because even crime fighters get days off and some of them even have special places they go to relax."

I knew what she meant. We always had a good time at the museum, which is kind of like the Batcave for Batman, except there were lots of other people walking around.

The museum trip started out fun. Then for some reason I thought I saw the big kid right there, in front of the fish tank, until the guy turned around and I saw he was someone else. I got all cold and shaky and felt like I couldn't move when that happened.

I told Joyce, and she said that was all a "natural reaction" and that your mind can trick you into imagining you see something you have been thinking hard about. She said it might even happen again and it would be a good idea for us to talk about that, if it ever did.

So we had a mostly okay day, but sometimes I couldn't help it and I would think back to the big kid's face being all angry or what else I saw and why did I even go with him to get the ball when I didn't know him.

I even thought about all those mixed up "Is he my boyfriend?" feelings and felt really mad at myself.

Joyce must have seen from my face that I was thinking unhappy things because she asked me what was wrong. I said, "I'm thinking back about the basketball trouble."

Joyce told me I could squeeze her hand as hard as I wanted any time my thinking flashed back to what happened.

I said,

"What about when your hand is not there?"

Joyce said, "We'll work on that. I have some ideas. But, for now, just squeeze my hand. You can squeeze it 'til it gets purple as a grape and I won't mind."

So, after that I squeezed her hand a couple of times and one time it did get kind of red like a strawberry and she said ouch, but then she laughed and gave me a big hug and I laughed, too.

The day after that, Joyce said, "Come here, I've got a present for you." She handed me a small jewelry box and inside was a necklace with a charm that looked very familiar. Joyce smiled and explained it to me:

"This is a copy of one of the most important medals ever awarded to anybody for great courage.

It's the same as the one the Cowardly Lion got in the *Wizard of Oz* movie."

That was my favorite movie in the whole world, except for maybe all the Harry Potters. Joyce explained she had to send away for it but the box was the one her wedding ring came in. That meant I now had two special treasures.

"I want you to wear this when I'm not around for purple hand squeezing," said Joyce, "You can touch it and remember that you are the hero.

"*You* are the crime fighter superhero in this story, the bravest of the brave, the proudest of the proud and the winner of the battle."

I knew that in the beginning of a story, it is always hard for the hero. They have to fight for what's right and solve a problem that seems bigger than they are.

Being brave is a good thing, but sometimes it feels almost too hard. You can have bad dreams, think bad thoughts, and remember awful parts.

Thinking and remembering can feel awful, sad, and scary or make me too angry to talk. That's when I look at my courage medal, to remember I am a hero and a crime fighter.

I still go to my Joyce for a good hand squeeze or a big hug. When I get really quiet and am by myself for a long time, she always asks me what I'm thinking and we talk about it until I feel better.

Or we decide not to talk and go do something else.

For me now it seems like a long time ago because now I'm in a different grade and older. It's kind of like I wrote my own story or made a movie in my head.

It's a movie I have seen again and again but I always know when the scary parts will come up and that I always, always, will save myself.

I don't feel like I am living inside the movie, which is how it was at first. Now it's more like I am watching someone else. Just like in the cartoons, she escapes. The girl in my movie is always a crime fighter and a hero.

The next day, Joyce told me it was time to do something with the white card the policeman gave us. This meant more "taking care of business." She said that someone had already called her but, since this was my business, I should do as much as I could by myself.

What did I need to do?

"We need to make an appointment for you to talk to the prosecutor about your case."

I was confused again. Who was that?

"After a crime has been committed, the people involved go to court. Two lawyers talk about what happened, they ask different people to come up and answer questions and then they talk about it in front of a judge."

"And a jury?" I asked. I saw this on TV.

"Sometimes a jury, but not this time because both you and that boy are under the age of 18. You are both still kids."

Thinking and remembering can feel awful, sad, and scary or make me too angry to talk. That's when I look at my courage medal, to remember I am a hero and a crime fighter.

It's a movie I have seen again and again, but I always know when the scary parts will come up and that I always, always will save myself.

"Do we both have lawyers?" This was on TV, too.

"Yes. Each side has a lawyer. Your lawyer has a regular name, Mr. Edward Kovach. But he also has a court name: The Prosecutor. Or Mr. Prosecutor. And the lawyer for the boy has a regular name but is also called a defense attorney, or 'the lawyer for the defendant.'"

"Shouldn't I be the 'defendant' because I defended myself?"

Joyce said, no because now I was safe and the boy was in trouble. His defense lawyer would try to defend him against punishment. The prosecutor would help me explain what happened and why the boy should be punished and why I should be protected. Mr. Kovach was part of my crime fighting team.

The boy being the defendant meant he would get a chance to answer questions about what happened and tell his side of the story to defend himself.

"Does that mean he'll make excuses because he got caught?" I asked Joyce.

"I would not be surprised," she said.

"But he really did do it," I said.

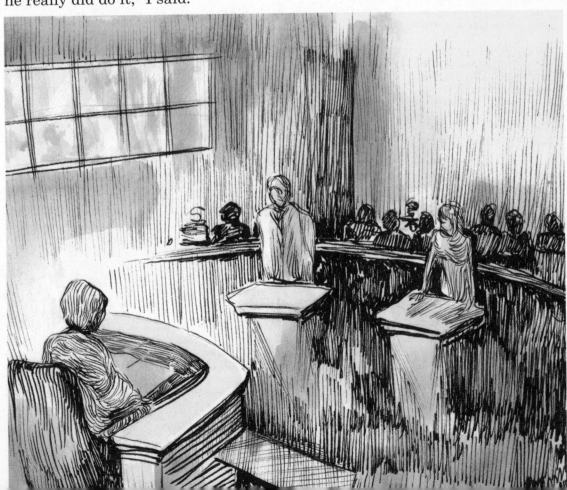

"Yes, he did. He did this to you without your permission. He broke the law. He has no defense. Even if he lies, we all know what really happened."

Joyce told me to call* the number on the card for Prosecutor Edward Kovach, to make our appointment. On the card, it said "Case Number:" with some numbers the policeman wrote in for us, before he gave us the card.

"Tell them your name and case number," said Joyce, "and tell them you are calling to make an appointment. We can come in any day except Wednesday afternoons when you have swim team at the pool."

I called the number and the woman who answered sounded very nice but a little bit confused.

She said, "I'm not sure I understand you. Are you saying to me that you are the victim? Is your mother there?"

I told her my Joyce was right there, but this was my business to take care of and I knew that some people would call me a victim but I really was a crime fighter and Mr. Edward Kovach was part of my team.

* Kids who have been victimized have had power taken away from them. The more such kids can do for themselves (make a phone call, help organize a Courage Party) the more they feel in control of their new circumstances, which can help return a sense of security to them.

Then I could hear her voice smiling through the phone and she told me I sounded like a very brave and remarkable girl and could I come in next Monday at 10am?

I said yes, we could and did I have to wear a dress or anything?

She laughed and said no, play clothes would be fine but if I had a school ID card, it would be good to have that with me. I said I would bring both my picture pool pass and my school ID and she said I should be sure to stop by her desk to say hello and that her name was Mrs. Linda Jenkins.

When we went to the courthouse, where Mr. Edward Kovach, Prosecutor, had his office (and his name on a gold plate on the door), we first had to go through a metal detector and the police lady looked in Joyce's purse.

I asked if it was okay that we brought snack bars and she said that was very smart because the vending machines just had cheese and crackers and candies that were older than she was! Joyce laughed and got her purse back and then we went to meet Mrs. Linda Jenkins.

Mrs. Jenkins was very friendly and she had little wrapped candies on her desk. She told me to help myself, but I should know the blue ones would turn my tongue blue. Then she stuck out her tongue to show me she had a blue tongue and winked at me. "Don't let that stop you from enjoying them, though!"

I put one in my pocket because I was getting that nervous feeling in my stomach again. I was worrying about what I would have to do and say when I met the prosecutor.

Mr. Kovach was almost as little as me! Or, at least it seemed like that because he sat in a wheelchair and rolled out to shake my hand. And that's when I saw he had no legs.

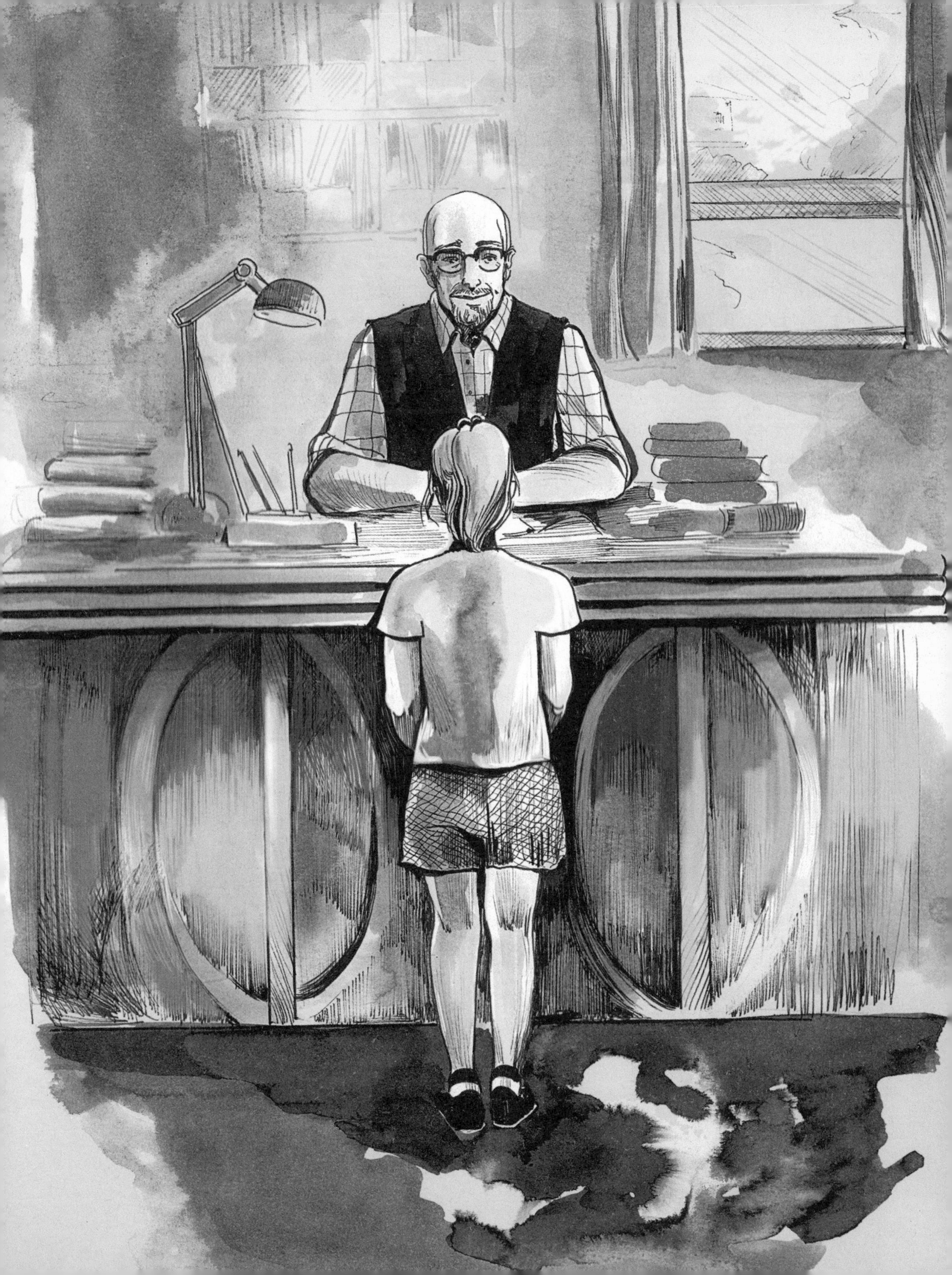

He saw me looking and I was embarrassed because it is not polite to stare and he told me right away that he became a lawyer because, when he was a kid even younger than me, he was the victim of a crime, like me.

"I was riding my bicycle home. A man who was driving drunk hit me and there went my legs! I liked the lawyer who prosecuted him so much that I decided to grow up to be just like her. So, I went to law school."

I thought this was a sort of happy ending, but not really, because he did not have any legs. Then he said, "We are both going to get to know each other very well and we are going to be talking about some things we usually keep private, almost secret. Like what happened to you in the park.

"In here, you and I are going to have no secrets. Not even about what happened to our bodies. So, let me tell you one of my most important body secrets: 'Not everybody in this courthouse knows I do not have any legs!'

This sounded very strange to me. Like very strange crazy, but I kept my mouth shut.

Then he told me to look behind his desk and there were two feet with shoes and socks on, attached to what looked like two plastic legs, like big human doll legs. And in the corner I saw he had two crutches.

He explained that most of the time he wore his legs, and no one could tell unless he wore shorts.

"But I like to take them off sometimes, when it is hot outside or when I sit down for a long time to work on my computer. And of course, I take them off when I play basketball!"

He grinned at me and then he showed me a picture of a whole bunch of guys and even two ladies in wheelchairs wearing shorts and jerseys. One guy was holding a basketball and another had a giant trophy.

"That's my team," he said. "We call ourselves the Demon Wheelers and last year we took the championship!"

I told him I thought the trophy looked very awesome and asked him what other sports he liked to play. He told me he liked to swim and play the drums, and he liked to make and fly kites with his kids, down by the lake.

"But, basketball is my game," he said. "Can you tell me what happened the day you went to the park to play basketball and met that boy?"

Here I was, expected to be telling the whole story again. Mr. Kovach smiled and said to take my time and that this was probably not going to be the last time I would be asked to tell my story but he had plenty of time to listen.

I said that I never knew crime fighters had to do so much talking and he laughed and said that not everyone got to ride in the Batmobile, at least not all the time, but what we did together here was very important and to expect him to ask lots of questions, because now we were a team.

Then, he reached in his drawer and gave me a pin that said "Demon Wheelers" and put another one on his shirt and said to me, "OK, Demon Wheeler Crime Fighter! Now that we are on the same team, let's get started."

I told him my whole story, again and again and then I answered some questions and went back over some parts of my story another time.

My mouth was getting tired so I asked if I could unwrap and eat my candy now and he said yes, and if I wanted, we could go to the vending machine but I said no thank you, because I knew the crackers and cheese here are antiques. He thought this was very funny and said "Right you are, Demon Wheeler Crime Fighter!"

And then he asked me about Michael, the kid from my school who was there and how I knew him. I told him I first met him at school and he sometimes went to the park or the pool but we didn't really hang out together because he had his own friends.

"Is he a nice boy?" Mr. Kovach asked.

I said he was just a boy and I really did not know but he didn't get into a lot of fights or start trouble at school, except he sometimes teased one of the popular girls in our class and called her Alien Space Monkey.

"That sometimes got him in trouble, like if the teacher heard," I explained. "But most of the time she just got back at him at recess, so it was all pretty even."

Mr. Kovach asked me if I knew Michael's last name, so I told him. And then he said he had something to tell me about the boy who attacked me.

I took a deep breath, because I really did not want to hear or talk about him much more because I already had to go through this a zillion times. But Mr. Kovach said this was important:

"The person who assaulted you has done this before. Let me show you something."

He pulled out a folder with the boy's name on it and some numbers. There were white, yellow, and pink papers inside. He showed me some words and began to explain them.

"Last year, he was brought to court for hurting a little girl even younger than you, in the same kind of way."

I told him that Dr. Anne was right! She thought maybe this could have happened. But why didn't he get stopped? Why did he go on to attack me?

"Dr. Anne is a smart lady," said Mr. Prosecutor Edward Kovach. "We have worked together before.

"In this folder is the whole story about another little girl we'll pretend is named Mia.

"There is a police report. There is a doctor's report with private pictures of what he did to her in this sealed envelope, that we will not open.

"There are witness statements: everything everybody who saw or knew about the crime, all written down, typed out, and signed.

"This boy tricked her into going somewhere alone with him and then he hurt her sexually. She could not fight back right away but her mother knew something was wrong because she came home crying."

I wondered if her mother let her pour water on her head to cool off. But then I saw the date and it was in the winter. So, maybe they just hugged.

"We had all the stories, everyone together, and were all set to get this guy," said Mr. Kovach. "But something happened, and this is what we ended up with."

He showed me a paper that had a bunch of long words and pointed to three words at the end that said,

"Dismissed with Prejudice."

I knew prejudice was something bad. Like we talk about in social studies about civil rights and Martin Luther King. But I did not understand. Mr. Kovach seemed to know that I was confused and he explained to me it had another meaning for courts and law.

"I am not sure why, but in the end the little girl never showed up. Maybe she was too scared to tell anyone in a courtroom about what happened. Or maybe her parents decided they wanted to just try to pretend nothing happened and forget about it. That happens."

I could kind of understand, but what about using her secret powers of truth and courage? And why would her family just try to pretend when everyone knew what happened?

"I do not know the answer to that," Mr. Kovach said. "The judge said that all we needed was for the little girl to come to court and tell us what everyone already knew. He wanted that big boy stopped.

"In the United States of America, anyone who is accused of committing a crime has the right to have the person who is accusing them of a crime face them in a courtroom. The accuser has to answer questions. It can't just be "He Said. She said.""

"'Dismissed with Prejudice' is a way of saying we all heard what really happened and were convinced he committed a crime but unless a victim speaks out, we have to let him go."

So he could do it again. To me. And maybe to other kids too scared to say anything. This made me feel really mad and scared all at the same time.

"I don't want him to do this again," I said. "That park is *our* park. It's a place where big and little kids can play. It is supposed to be safe."

Mr. Kovach said, "Taking care of creeps like him is the best way we know how to keep everybody safe. That, and learning some other ways to protect yourself.

"You did a lot of things that were very right, like yelling and yelling and fighting back and running to safe grownups and then calling the police and talking to them and giving them a good description.

"What you told them about his underwear was absolutely spot on. The police saw his underwear, too, and that will help us prove you are right!"

"So everybody will know then that he did it, and then it will be over?" I asked.

"Even though he knows what he did to you, we can expect him to say nothing happened. He will try to lie to get out of it. And other people might lie, too."

I thought about his mother who kept yelling, "My boy is a good boy!"

"The other lawyer in the courtroom will be a defense lawyer who will be completely and totally on his side and will ask you some questions that may confuse you or even bother you.

"Just stick to the truth. If you do not know an answer, do not try to make anything up just to come up with an answer.

"A courtroom is not school and the defense lawyer is not a teacher you are trying to please.

"Think of the defense lawyer as part of his family, someone who is totally fooled into thinking he is a wonderful boy and that you are a terrible liar."

I know parents like that. Like when Shannon stole a candy bar and got caught and lied to her mom. Her mom did the "My girl is a good girl!" thing and tried to put it on me until the cash register lady said no, she'd seen me outside the whole time, watching our bikes and it was all Shannon.

I asked my prosecutor lawyer if he and the defense lawyer would do a lot of yelling, like on TV and he said, no they usually tried to keep it quiet.

Then he told me how important it would be for me to be able to say yes, the boy in the courtroom chair was the one who did it.

"Do not be surprised if he looks very different when he shows up. He will probably have on a nice suit and a new haircut and, for some reason, a lot of these guys show up wearing fake glasses.

I think they do that to try to look like they are good students who do not make trouble or get into fights."

I said I knew about disguises. Clark Kent wears glasses and a suit so no one can tell he is Superman. And he pretends to be very shy while he works hard to write the best stories for the newspaper. But I always know that he is Superman.

When we were finally finished talking about our whole crime fighting plan against the boy who attacked me, Mr. Kovach told me, "The next time I see you, I will be wearing my legs

and my Demon Wheelers button. You can wear yours, too, so you can remember we are a team.

"Anytime you get confused or even a little nervous or scared in the courtroom, you look at me. Look at my face or look for my Demon Wheelers button. When you see that, it will remind you we are both champions!"

Mr. Kovach told me there was someone else I was going to meet today but no, that person would not be asking me so many questions because she already understood what had happened to me.

He told me she was outside, talking to Joyce, and that she would be my advocate from the Rape Crisis Center.

"I will let Caitlin tell you more about the Rape Crisis Center where she works, when you meet her. Do you know what an advocate is?"

I said no. It sounded like "avocado" and I hoped it was something nice.

"An advocate is a trusted adult who will stick to your side through this whole business and try to make everything go as easily as possible for you and your family, until the end."

I explained that I already had an adult friend guardian named Joyce who stuck by my side and Mr. Kovach nodded and smiled.

"Yes," he said "And I think she has been doing a splendid job but remember, we are building a championship crime fighting team for you and we can always use an extra player. Caitlin is a true champion and I think you will really like her."

Caitlin had very short hair, very blue eyes, very pretty feather earrings and a bird tattoo on the muscle of her arm. She was talking to Joyce outside and they were laughing. When she met me, she said,

"Wow! I am always proud to meet another kid who fought back. Not everybody gets the chance to do that right away. Sometimes they have to wait until they get all the way to this office. But you hit the ground running!"

I said, yes I did do a lot of running and I ended up pouring water on my head at the end.

"Just like a marathon racer," said Caitlin. "That was good. And Joyce tells me that you are going to have a party to celebrate your courage. Very good. All very good."

Then Caitlin told me about her job. She said the Rape Crisis Center helps people who were attacked sexually: adults and kids. She said they also help families understand what happened and how to help.

They try to prevent sexual assault with special classes about self-defense and other things. Most importantly, they go with victims to see doctors or the police or to court and wherever else they were needed.

I said I was more like a crime fighter than a victim and she said she wished more people had my attitude. Then she said that the first thing she was going to do would be to show me what it looked like in a courtroom.

She said we could tiptoe in the back and watch a real judge and some lawyers in a court case that had to do with someone crashing a car, and we did.

It wasn't very interesting. The judge was wearing black but he did not look as big as I thought he would and he seemed kind of bored.

He asked the man sitting next to him some questions and then he talked to two people in suits who were standing up. They were the lawyers, but I was not sure which side.

He hit his hammer one time, but it did not make a loud noise like on TV. Caitlin said that meant it was all over and I asked what happened and she said the insurance companies would have to figure out about fixing the smashed car.

Then we went into an empty courtroom and Caitlin showed me where everyone would be sitting and how, if I sat up next to the judge, I would have a microphone to speak into, so we practiced having me sit there and say my name and address into the microphone.

Caitlin showed me where Mr. Kovach would sit and where the boy and his lawyer would sit. I said I hoped my judge would not be bored and she said no, she knew who the judge would be and he would be very interested.

After that, Caitlin and Joyce and I went to a place she knew that had very good smoothies and we sat down to talk.

Caitlin told me that there was a special club at the Rape Crisis Center where kids could learn how to protect themselves and make art, dance, and do music and sit around and talk and do all kinds of other interesting things, including take field trips.

I asked where the field trips went and Caitlin said sometimes they go to the rec center to work out or watch karate classes and if we did that, she would be there wearing her white karate suit and her black belt because, guess what? She was also one of the karate teachers and had been practicing for years.

"We also go watch the roller derby girls skate in matches. When they push each other around the rink we cheer for our team, the Burning River Roller Girls. We get to blow off steam and scream a lot and the skaters love it."

I told Caitlin I liked to rollerblade and could scream very loud and Joyce said, "Oh, yes! She can." So, we made a date for me to go visit the kids club, which turned out to be very interesting and kind of fun, although sometimes we talked about bad stuff that had happened to us that we all agreed to keep secret and not leave the room.

So, I can't tell you about other kids' stories here (just mine) except to say most people would be very surprised to hear some of what happens to some kids and how grownups should really listen more and that you sometimes have to keep telling different grownups until you get to the one who will help and believe you.

There are Rape Crisis Centers with different names all over the country and you can find out their number if you look on the Internet or call 411.

If you call a Rape Crisis Center* you can talk to a good grownup.

You do not have to tell them your real name until you feel like you trust them.

You can call late at night, when no one in your house is listening.

They are there to understand, no matter what, and not blame you. They can tell you what to do next, how to start to make things better and get you safe.

They know how to talk "grownup-to-grownup" if you need help explaining what has been going on to good people in your family or anyone else, like police or doctors.

The best thing of all is that you can always call them back, especially if you get too nervous to talk the first time you call.

After Joyce and I finished talking to Caitlin, we went to the party store to buy balloons and paper streamers to decorate Reverend Peggy's room for my Courage Party. So, I think it's time to call this part of the book . . .

* Some numbers you can call are in the back of this book. Look up the number for your local Rape Crisis Center. There is a place for you to write it down in this book.

PART TWO:
HOW WE CELEBRATED MY TRUTH AND COURAGE

Before we left Caitlin at the smoothie shop, she said "Be sure to tell me all about how your Courage Party goes because I think it is a wonderful idea for people to celebrate kids' courage and be open about what happened, instead of giving kids 'conflicting messages.'"

I said, I did not know what "conflicting messages" were and she said that was something the kids talked about at the club because nearly everybody got those, instead of something as nice as my Cowardly Lion courage medal.

And, because I went to the kids' club later, I can sort of explain this to you now, as long as I don't tell anyone's private business.

A conflicting message is what happens when someone, usually a grownup, says to do or think one thing but you kind of know they don't really stick to what they say.

Like if they say don't ever swear and then they do, because they are in the car and traffic is really bad. If you catch them, sometimes they laugh.

Other times they might say "Mind your own business. Do what I say and not what I do." Your understanding gets pulled in two different directions.

Some of the kids in my group got told by their parents, "You have nothing to be ashamed about. You did not do anything wrong."

That is true. But, then they get a "conflicting message" and that mixes them up because, right after they are told not to be ashamed, they get told "Do not tell anyone!"

Which makes them feel they really should be ashamed.

Or, maybe they were told, "It was not your fault. No one is mad at you" but then, at night they can hear their parents yelling or even worse, crying about what happened.

Another conflicting message can be when everyone in the family seems angry or sad or ashamed anyway and there are a lot of whispers and rules about who in your family can know and who can't, like you can tell your doctor but don't tell your grandparents or even your best friend.

Caitlin and Joyce both think that if another kind of bad crime happened to kids, like someone pushed them over and stole their bike, or if they were beat up by bad kids who took their lunch money and cellphone, that no parent would keep that a secret.

I think they're right because when that happened to Justin, I know his mother went to school and told everybody and kept talking and talking about his lunch money and his cellphone until he was kind of embarrassed. If a kid came to school with a band-aid or a cast, they would tell everyone what happened and get a whole lot of attention.

If a girl fought back against another kind of criminal assault, like if someone grabbed her purse, everybody would give her a high five, or say how brave she was and not a wimp because she did her best to fight, even if she didn't win.

Maybe she would get a party. Maybe she would get flowers or a sticker. Or just a thumbs up or a hug from their teacher.

"Unlike criminal assault, sexual assaults have stigma," Caitlin told us in our group. "That means sexual assault is treated differently, like a big bad secret by a lot of grownups who really are not being very grownup and fair, after all. Why do you think that is?"

We all had different answers. Some kids thought it was because of how grandparents were sometimes very strict about things, like what kind of music or TV shows were okay or what kind of clothes were allowed.

Some said it was part of their religion or about nakedness. I told them Joyce said some adults were very nervous about sex, even after they did it and had kids.

Caitlin said those were all good answers and that the important thing was for us, who had things like this happen, to know how to erase the stigma, so we all took turns writing bad things people could say about us on the blackboard.

Then we took turns erasing them and writing in what we thought the real truth was or what we would say and think instead.*

One girl was very brave and said she had already heard someone say, "I bet you liked it. I bet you want to do it again."

That made her run home and cry a secret cry in her bedroom. So, we came up with lots of good answers for her to say out loud or at least put in her head to think instead, like:

---

* It helps to role play good answers and comebacks together. Take turns being the "mean kid" so you can listen to what your child is afraid they will hear.

You are just being mean and stupid. No one likes to be attacked. You can't make me feel ashamed of what happened to me. I am a brave crime fighter and a hero for telling the police a crime was committed against me.

(That one was my idea!)

You are ignorant. You are just trying to make me feel small because you think that makes you feel big and important. Your tricks don't work on me.

Go home and talk to your mother. Tell her you said that and listen to what she tells you.

You must be getting all your ideas from other dumb kids and dumb TV and dumb music. Make fun of me all you want, but you are acting like an ignorant kid. I know more about the real world than you do.

What happened to me could also happen to you and if it did I would not be acting all stupid and mean like you are now.

I had my chance to use some of our anti-stigma blackboard ammunition later that week when I went to the pool.

There was Michael, the kid I know who saw me at the park, and he came up to me with this mean little smile on his face and said in a singsong voice,

"Ha, ha! I know what happened to you in the woods with that guy!"

But Joyce and I had already practiced our "anti-stigma verbal ammunition" at home, with her being the rude guy, and right away I made my voice sound strong and confident and said,

"Yes, I went with him to get the ball. He tricked me and tried to hurt me, but I fought back and got away. He could have tricked you and hurt you, too.

"Anyway, for my courage I got this necklace and I'm having a party to celebrate how brave I am to get him caught and kicked out of the park for being a dangerous attacker.

"AND! Me and my guardian and my entire crime fighting team are going to kick his butt in court because he also did this to another kid littler than us, a girl just as old as your baby sister, so it is up to us to protect her because the park belongs to us kids—not *predators*!"

(I know what "predator" means. It means someone who watches and then hurts kids. Or an ugly creature who attacks and hurts aliens, like in "Alien VS. Predator" where the predators look as mean and dangerous as they really are, instead of like ordinary people, like they do here on Earth.)

Anyway, that word "predator" got Michael's attention, because I knew he had the Predator video game and he said "Oh!"

Then he thought about what I said and asked if he could see my necklace and he asked if it was solid gold and I said I did not care what it was made of, I cared about what it meant and it meant I was awarded the Medal of Courage for being brave and truthful.

Michael asked how he could get a medal, too.

I said I did not know, but he could be my hero by being truthful if he told everybody the real truth about what happened:

It could have happened to anyone and I'm the one who fought back and was okay now, and I was being a crime fighter to protect other kids from the big boy who had used our basketball game to try and get close to and hurt one of us kids.

I told Michael how the big boy hurt the girl I promised to call Mia. She was too little and scared to fight back. Maybe people said mean things and teased her until she felt ashamed and hid in her room instead of going to court. Because of this, the big boy got away and went after more kids.

That's why I was going to court to protect us all, especially the little kids. Nothing Michael or anyone else could say could make me feel embarrassed or ashamed, just mad about how totally ignorant or mean some people get because what happened was a *sexual* criminal assault instead of a plain *criminal* assault.

Michael said the police had asked him some questions and then his mom got a letter saying he would have to go to court to be a witness to tell what he saw or "witnessed" that day. She was not very happy about that.

I said here could be his chance to be a hero in another way, by telling the truth about what he saw in court.

I said I thought his mom would understand more if Michael told her about the little "Mia" and that this guy was the kind of predator who could hurt his baby sister, too, if he had the chance.

I said not to tell his baby sister about predators, not even for a joke to try to scare her, because she was very little and this was about real and serious danger.

Michael said he wouldn't because he would be in big trouble if he even tried to scare her with his plastic action figure Predator because his mom would take it away.

I told Michael I would be glad to see him at the courthouse and his mom could ask my advocate Caitlin or even Mr. Kovach or Joyce about all this. Good grownups can always talk in grownup language to other grownups.

The good grownups at the Rape Crisis Center can help other grownups understand what's going on, and you can find them by calling 411 or by searching online for "Rape Crisis Center near me."

After our talk, we jumped in the water with the other kids and played Marco Polo.

On the day of my Courage Party, we went early to Reverend Peggy's special room and she let us in and gave me a very big hug. She said she was so glad to see that I was okay and that she had her special story for me all ready and she was glad to be here because what happened made her think and she liked thinking.

I asked what kind of a special story and Joyce explained that each Courage Party lady was coming prepared to tell a special story from their own life and that I would be the first one to tell my own story about my brave day at the park and my crime fighting plan.

Mrs. Kent came, Dr. Anne came, Kaffers came, and Reverend Peggy was there. Everyone liked the decorations and the amazing picture Cory put on our cake. She made the super powered Japanese anime girl look like me, with all blonde hair and a ponytail.

We had blue and green decorations, plates and cups and blue and green sodas because those were my favorite colors and everyone put the food they brought on the blue and green paper tablecloths we put on the table.

There was a chair for each of us in a circle, with one in the middle.

Then I saw there were presents wrapped up for me, which they gave me right away. Reverend Peggy gave me sparkly blue and green shoelaces so I could run my fastest whenever I had to and Mrs. Kent gave me new blue and green sneakers that fit right away, because she asked Joyce what my size was.

She also laced up my sneakers with my new laces in a special way, the same as professional runners do and she told me how a long time ago, she had won track and field medals for races at school.

Being able to run fast can be really important, she said, and I knew just what she meant.

Kaffers gave me a sparkly, princessy magic wand and said she hoped I could use it to wish away any scary memories I might ever have about what happened.

I could see she was crying when she said that and I felt bad until Joyce said she was crying because she was happy. It was okay and I remembered how Kaffers always cried at movies, even Disney cartoons when there was a happy ending. Kaffers nodded and said, "That's me! The Public Waterworks!" and everybody laughed.

From Dr. Anne I got a book about sex and how your body grows up that had funny pictures in it, especially of the boy sperms all chasing a girl egg, where the sperms looked kind of like Casper the Friendly Ghost.

Then she surprised me with a superhero cape that had my name on the back in gold letters.

I put it on and said when I wasn't wearing it to fight crime, maybe I could wear it when I went rollerblading and draw tattoos on my arm muscles so I would look like one of the Burning River Roller Derby girls.

Dr. Anne said she thought that would be awesome and she liked the idea of girls getting stronger and stronger and that some of those derby girls were really buff Amazons, which made everyone laugh.

I said I knew that Wonder Woman came from an entire island full of Amazons who used magic ropes to make criminals tell the truth.

Then Joyce said, "So here we are, every one of us an Amazon and ready to welcome young Danielle into this circle of Amazons, because of her amazing heroic adventure.

"We are here to listen to her tell her own brave story and to celebrate and praise her for her Amazon truthfulness and courage, the weapons she will use as a crime fighter when she goes to court to protect herself and other children from a predator.

"No matter what happens in court, we are here to tell her we believe her story and stand by her. She has everyone's phone number on this card we all signed for her so she can call any of us any time she wants to, even at night, because we are here to listen and help and we are all on Danielle's team."

I think Joyce said more stuff like that in a very dramatic actress voice because Joyce sometimes writes for plays or movies, but I can't remember it all.

It was a pretty good speech that made me feel like the star of a show who won the prize, and it felt nice but also a little embarrassing to be the center of attention.

When Joyce sat down, I saw I was not finished being the center of attention because there I was in the middle with everyone saying they wanted to hear all about my brave deed. So, I had to tell my story again but this time it was sort of different.

All the women kind of told it with me, by making sounds and clapping and pounding on their thighs and chests and saying different things that cheered me on. So, it wasn't a serious or sad retelling of my story. It was like we were a tribe or team, with everyone in the room all on the same side with me.

When I got to the part where the boy was taking over our game, someone said "Uh, oh . . . I smell a tricky rat! Why isn't he playing ball with the kids his own age on the other court? Did anyone know this guy? Was he someone's big brother?"

And others said, "Boo! Here comes the creep! Look out, kids! Is he a stranger big kid? Did you know him?"

When we got to where I thought he might be talking about being my boyfriend, I was a little embarrassed. And that's when Mrs. Kent said,

"It's okay to be interested in boys. You are going to have plenty of guys wanting to be your boyfriend when the time comes.

"You'll know what's going on, no question about it.

"The right person will adore you because of your brains and courage, and you will have no trouble picking the best person for you. You will never settle for a creep!"

All the women whistled and clapped and said "Uh HUH!" and "Yes, indeed!"

When we got to the part where he pulled his pants down, they all said, "Ew! Gross! How rude! Get away from that guy!"

When I was fighting to be free, everyone cheered for me. When I told about the running, they were all inside my story with me, saying "Run! Run! Go, Dani! You can do it!"

Everybody laughed when I told about pouring the water on my head and Joyce yelled out like a baseball umpire, "Safe! Our girl is safe because she is the bravest, strongest, fastest, smartest, best kid in the world!"

Joyce can get a little over the top but, for that moment with everyone cheering and clapping and hugging me, I really did feel all brave and important.

After that, I told them about Mr. Kovach and going to court and having to sit in the chair up high, next to the judge and tell my story.

Everyone was interested and Kaffers said she was going to come with us, wearing a suit and carrying her briefcase so she would look all official. Everyone else said they would do the same thing and they would look like a Dream Team: a whole bunch of ferocious women who all knew how to take care of business and be on my side.

I got to cut my cake then and everybody's lips turned blue and green from the icing, so we had to use a lot of napkins to try to wash it off and Joyce had a lipstick in her purse, so she put that on my mouth. That made everyone laugh, because now I had pink lips with a blue and green outline all around.

"Now it is time for each of us to tell you a story from our own lives," said Joyce in her big dramatic stage actress voice, again.

"I call upon Reverend Peggy, she of the blue and green lips to tell our Danielle a true to life story that will lend perspective to the matter at hand!"

Then Joyce used her real Joyce voice and explained, "We have all had different experiences that we want to share with you, to help you better understand what happened to you.

"Lending perspective means sharing stories that connect to your story, but told from our own point of view or perspective."

I figured out for myself that "the matter at hand" was just another way of saying what we were there for, and Joyce said yes and that was just her way of imitating the fancy language I would hear in court.

Everybody agreed that I should always remember to not be afraid to ask what any words meant, especially when I was in court, because I was going to be the Star Witness, the most important person there and not him. I said I already knew words like defendant and prosecutor and now I was ready to hear Reverend Peggy's story, which went like this:

REVEREND PEGGY'S STORY

"When you got to the part where you poured the ice water on your head, I thought 'Wow! I know just how she felt!'" said Reverend Peggy, as she sat down in the center, in the storytelling chair and I took her seat. "Because once I had to go a long way home by myself. I would have poured ice water on my head then, too, because just like you I was boiling mad."

When I was in high school, I went to the prom with a boy my cousin introduced me to. We did not know each other well, but I had a good time until after the prom and he was driving me home.

He did not drive me straight home. Instead, he drove us out into the middle of a cornfield and stopped the car. I was starting to feel a little nervous, because I had to be home by a certain time. Also, I was having this tingly feeling in my chest and stomach. It was not a good tingle. It was the one I get, even today, when I know something is kind of wrong and there might be trouble. Does anyone else ever get that kind of feeling?*

* What does it feel like to YOU when something dangerous starts to happen?

Everyone else said yes, they did and when that nervous kind of worried feeling shows up, listen to it! It usually is a special kind of warning to be careful and pay attention to what is happening in case of danger.

I said that I don't get a tingle, but my hands turn very cold and even get damp. Peggy nodded.

"It's good to know about your own private distant early warning system, Danielle. I'll bet it helped you be aware of what was happening when that boy pulled your hair and pulled his pants down. You knew at once what was wrong and were able to move fast."

She continued, "When I looked over at my date, I saw that he had unbuttoned his pants and was holding his penis in his hand. I had never seen a grownup penis before, just my baby brother in the bathtub. And I did not want to look at his penis.

I did not want to touch his penis when he told me to touch it. It is okay to touch a penis if the penis is attached to someone you like and they ask you nicely to touch their penis and you have already decided that you want to touch their penis.

But you never, ever, have to touch a penis you do not want to touch. I told him no, but he kept trying to get me to touch his penis so I got out of the car.

I walked all the way home through the cornfield and it was a long walk that ruined my party shoes and dress, but I did not care!

The only time you should ever touch a penis is if that's what you want to do, when you are grown up, and when the person who the penis belongs to is someone you know and love, like a husband or a boyfriend.

Oh, my! Reverend Peggy said "penis" twelve times and she did not seem to be embarrassed at all.

I was glad she told me that story, using the correct word instead of a baby word like "wee-wee" because that way we all understood what she was talking about and it was a serious word for a serious story.

Everyone clapped at the end and Mrs. Kent even said "Amen to that, sister!" which made everyone laugh and clap even more.

Then it was time for Mrs. Kent to tell her story.

I walked all the way home
through the cornfield and it
was a long walk that ruined
my party shoes and dress, but
I did not care!

MRS. KENT'S STORY

I already told you that something happened to me when I was little and that I never told anyone, except my mother, until I was grown.

At first, my mother refused to believe what I said. She told me I was a nasty troublemaker and a liar, because the person who was hurting me was in our family.

He was her brother, my uncle, and this all happened to me when we were living in his house. My mom was trying to get a job, because my dad left and was not even paying child support.

So we were living with Uncle for free, except when my mom got some money from cleaning houses or babysitting and most of that went to him.

He would make fun of her for not making enough money. She was always very afraid he would kick us out and we would have nowhere to go. It was like we all had to do what he said, no matter what, even my mom.

Whatever he did, like when he was drunk and being very mean, we had to put up with it until we could get our own place.

That's why, when he first started to molest me, which means to sexually bother and hurt me, I tried to keep it to myself.

He also said that if I told anybody he would hurt my little sister, and I knew I had to protect her.

My mother would babysit, and I hated it when she left, even though that is how she got money for our new backpacks and sneakers.

I would rather have gone to school with a garbage bags for my books, wearing my old flip flops even in the winter because what my uncle would do to me when she was gone was so awful. But I kept my mouth shut because my sister was really little and I thought I was the only one who could protect her.

Finally, one day my mom saw some blood in my underpants and she was sure I was starting to have my period already.* So I told her the truth: that it was from him hurting me.

She got really mad. He was her brother and she had known him all her life and I was always starting trouble and we had to go along with him because where else would we live.

She said I was a liar and to never talk about it again. Then she gave me some menstrual pads.

---

* This is a good place to ask if your child has any questions about what a period is.

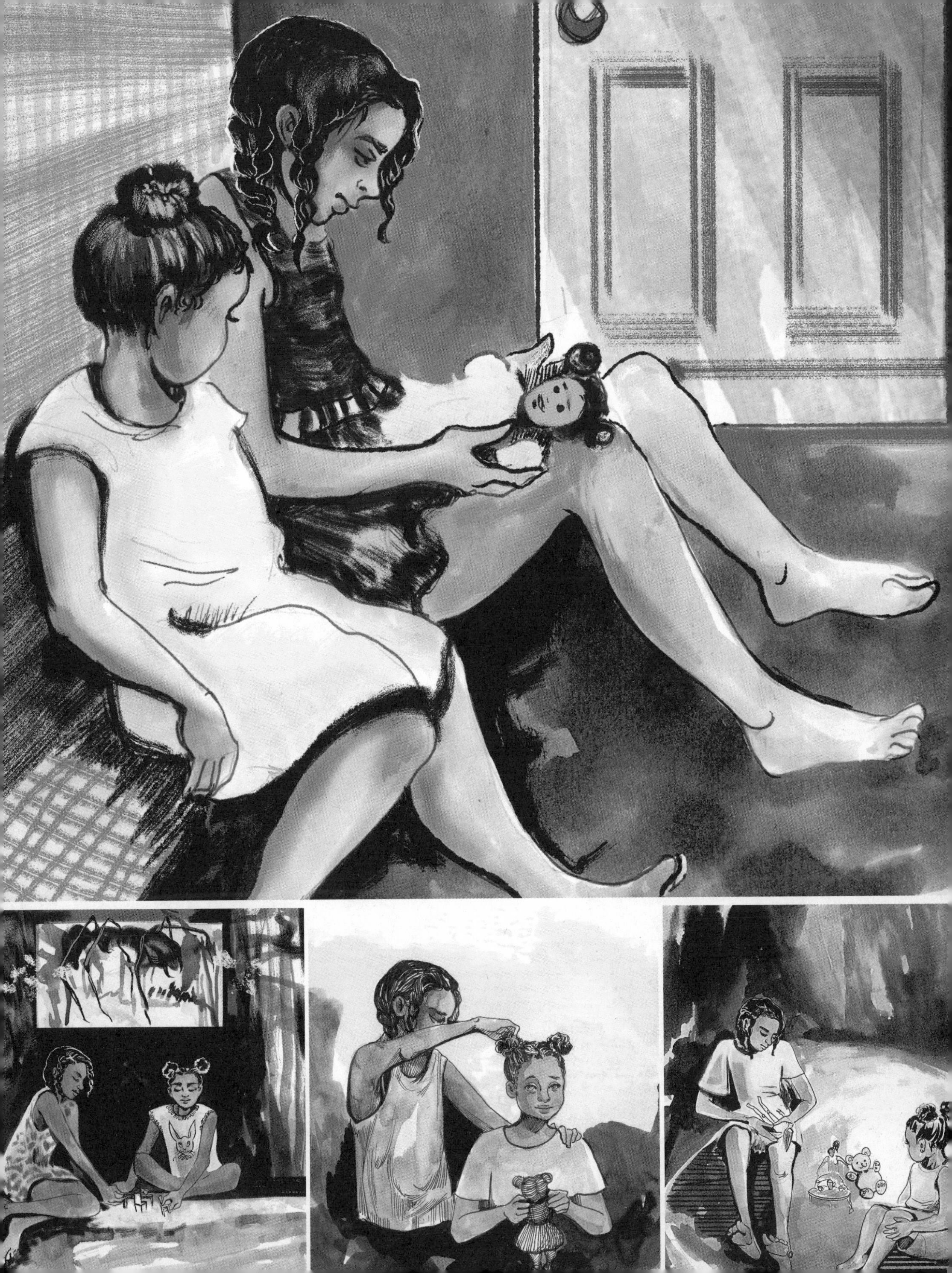

That was the scariest, loneliest time of my life. I have never felt as terrible as I did that day.

And I did not know then how kids like me should keep telling and telling other grownups until they find a good grownup who listens.

I could have told my gym teacher. I could have told our pastor's wife, who was very nice. I could have told my school counselor. I could have told the mother of one of my good friends.

I could have told a lot of people.

Instead, I shut up and soon after that his hurting me with "Our Special Game" stopped. I tried to forget all about it, even though I always felt sick when we ate with him at the table.

I pushed the whole thing down inside me and tried not to think about it until, one day, I was helping my little sister go potty and I saw blood in her underpants.

I was so scared and angry! I asked her what happened and she said Uncle hurt her when they were playing "Our Special Game" and did she have to do it again? He said he would cut off all her hair and then kill me, if she didn't do what he said and didn't keep quiet.

I put my arms around her and we went to hide in our bedroom closet, where I put toys for her to play with and a pillow and our little pink trash can, in case we had to go potty while we were hiding.

He never came looking for us, but I was ready in case he did. I had Mom's sharp metal nail file and my baseball bat for protection.

When Mom came home, she looked and looked and then finally found us. I told her about my sister and showed Mom her panties. I said he had promised not to hurt her if I played "Our Special Game" and asked if that was what I had to do again, to protect her and have a home . . .

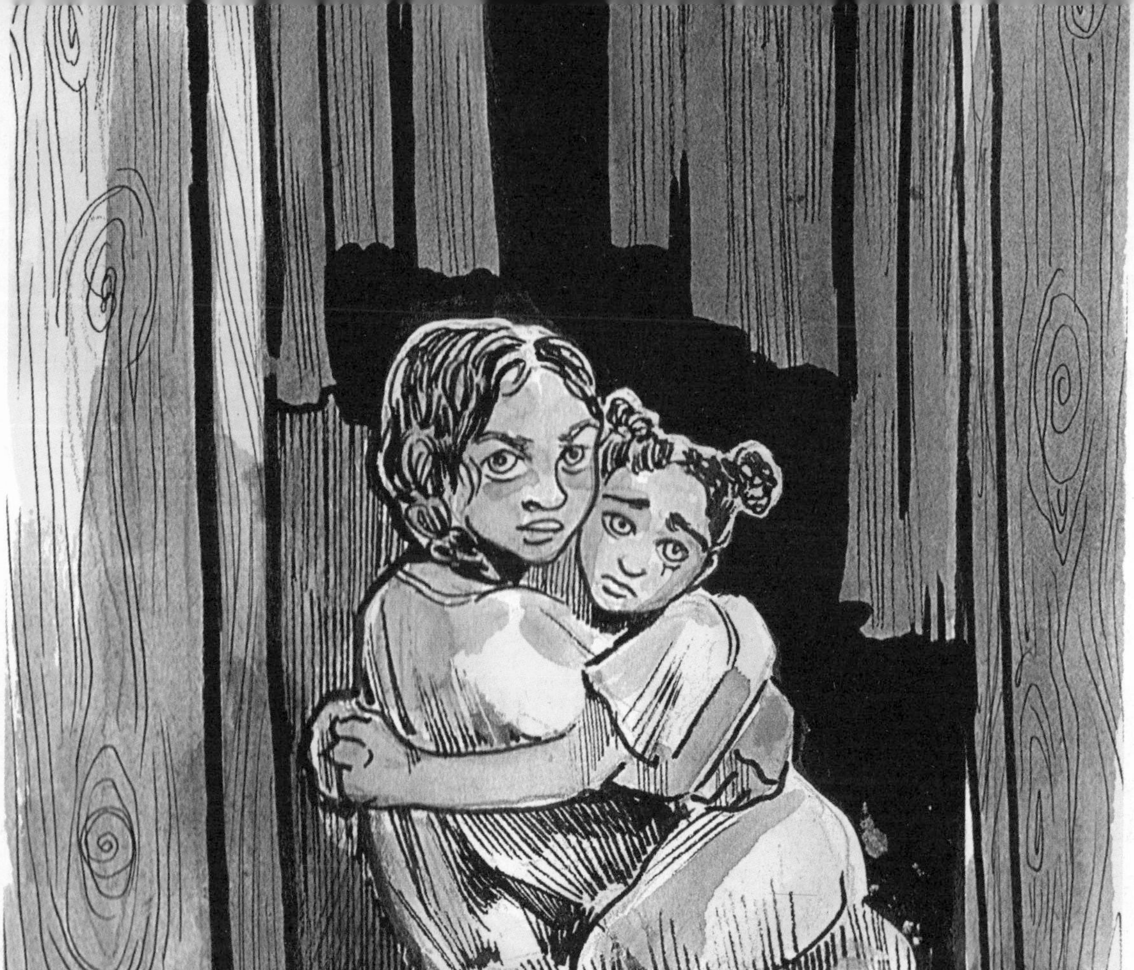

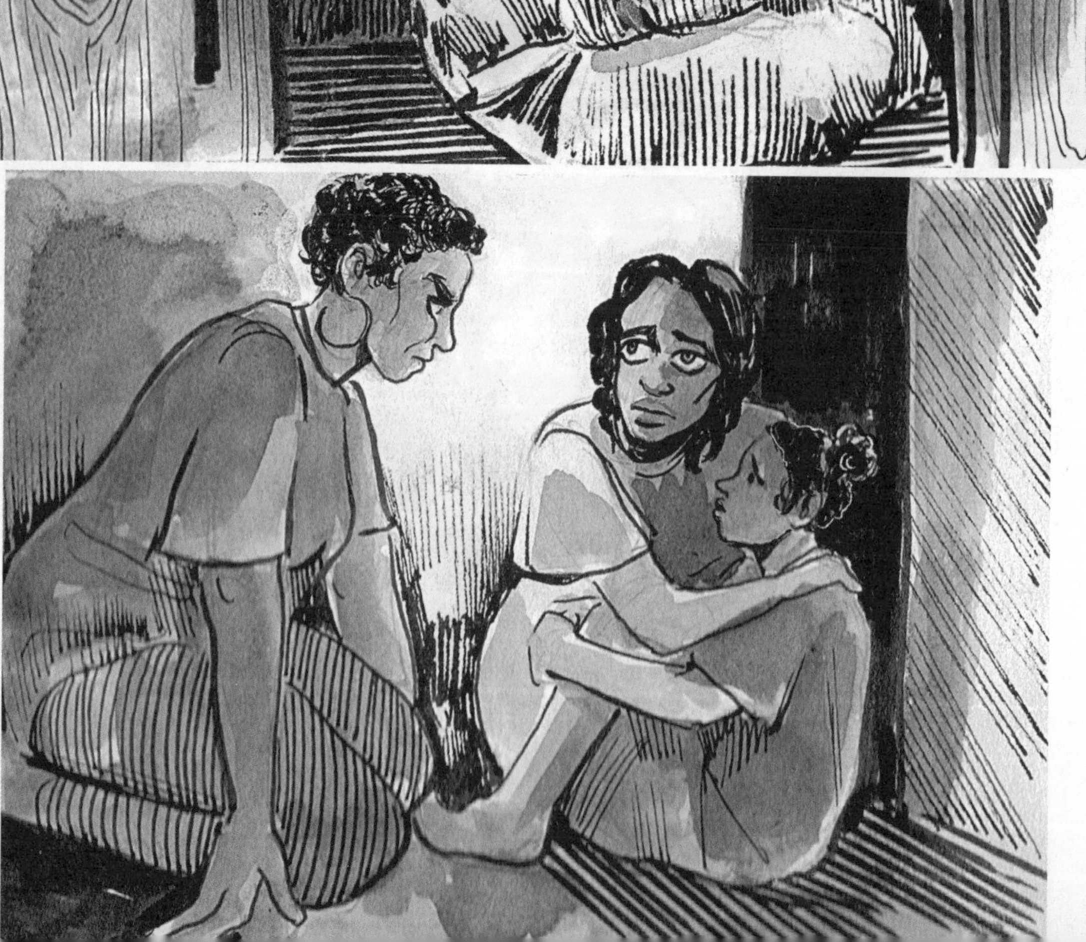

Mom stopped me there and said "No!" very loudly. She said to quickly pack our clothes in our backpacks because she believed me now and we were going to leave right away.

She kept her babysitting money this time and we went to stay in a motel, where we each had our own towel and a little cake of soap. Mom was crying in her eyes, but not out loud because there were so many things she had to do. She made some phone calls.

After that, we took a bus to another city, where Mom had a friend who let us stay there.

That was when Mom said to never, ever tell anyone what happened and that it was all behind us. It was an ugly secret that would get me in trouble if I told anyone and that I should never talk about it to her or to my little sister again, because we wanted her to forget.

Mom got a job where her friend worked, cleaning office buildings, and soon we got our own place. We never saw my uncle and we never talked about it, but it always bothered me and sometimes I had nightmares that brought it all back.

I went to college and shared a room there with my best friend. She saw I was having nightmares and asked me what's up?

I finally told her and she said that was a rotten thing to do to a kid, to shut them up when they needed to talk, and there was a counselor at the college who might be able to help me. She walked me to my first appointment.

The counselor was very nice and later I met a group of girls my age who met at the local Rape Crisis Center, like your kids group.

They said it did not matter that it had happened to me a long time ago. They told me I was very brave for protecting my sister the real way—not by going along with him, but my keeping her safe in the closet and continuing to try to make my mom understand, even though it seemed like she did not want to at first.

Parents make mistakes and sometimes they do not listen right away. But I knew that night back then that, if Mom didn't listen, I was going to take my sister somewhere safe the next morning. Maybe to the library, maybe to my teacher at school.

Back then I did not know how to call 911 or how to explain what was going on to a dispatcher. Or what a Rape Crisis Center is and how to find them online. I'm glad that's something kids can do today.

I'm okay about this now, but I wish someone had given me a Courage Party. It would have made me feel better and not so ashamed. Because I had nothing to be ashamed of.

And I *did* talk to my little sister after going to the counselor. She had remembered it all that time and was very glad to talk to me about it. When she came to visit me at college, she went with me to my girls group and we talked to my counselor together.

When Mrs. Kent finished her story, I said this could be her Courage Party too, and also Revered Peggy's and that tomorrow I would get out my art supplies and make them both *Congratulations on Your Courage!* cards so they would feel celebrated.

Everyone liked that idea and Joyce said what we all had in common was knowing how to use our powers of truth and courage.

Then it was time for Dr. Anne's story.

DR. ANNE'S STORY

The story I am going to tell you is not very long, but I think it will teach you something about self-protection: Personal safety rules do *not* change, no matter where you are.

I forgot those rules, when I was a young woman traveling by myself in another country, with my backpack. It is always better to take trips like that with a partner, but the girl I was traveling with went home early, so I was on my own.

It was late at night and I had missed the bus to the hostel where I would be staying.

A hostel is like a very inexpensive hotel for young travelers. You bring your own sleeping bag and sleep in a dormitory with other kids. Often hostels have special rules. Doors get locked at a certain time at night and do not get opened until the morning.

That is what happened to me. I had to walk and walk and my backpack was very heavy. I was exhausted when I arrived and the doors were locked! No one would be there to let me in until the morning.

I sat down in the doorway, thinking I would have to sit on the steps until morning.

Then a young man my own age came along and saw me. He could speak English! He asked me what was wrong and, after I told him, he said I could come home with him and his mother would fix me a place to stay.

I went home with him. He carried my backpack for me and I thought I was very lucky. Then, when I got inside his house, I realized he had lied. There was no mother. There was no extra bed.

He expected me to have sex with him, in exchange for having a place to sleep. He was a stranger who tricked me into going with him, just like what happened to you, Danielle.

I had forgotten something important: Personal safety rules do *not* change, no matter where you are. Do not go off alone with strangers, not in the United States, not in your own neighborhood, and not anywhere else.

It was a bad situation for me to be in. When I finally got away from him, I went back to the hostel and stayed there until it opened. In the girls' dormitory, I cried and cried and the other girls were very nice to me.

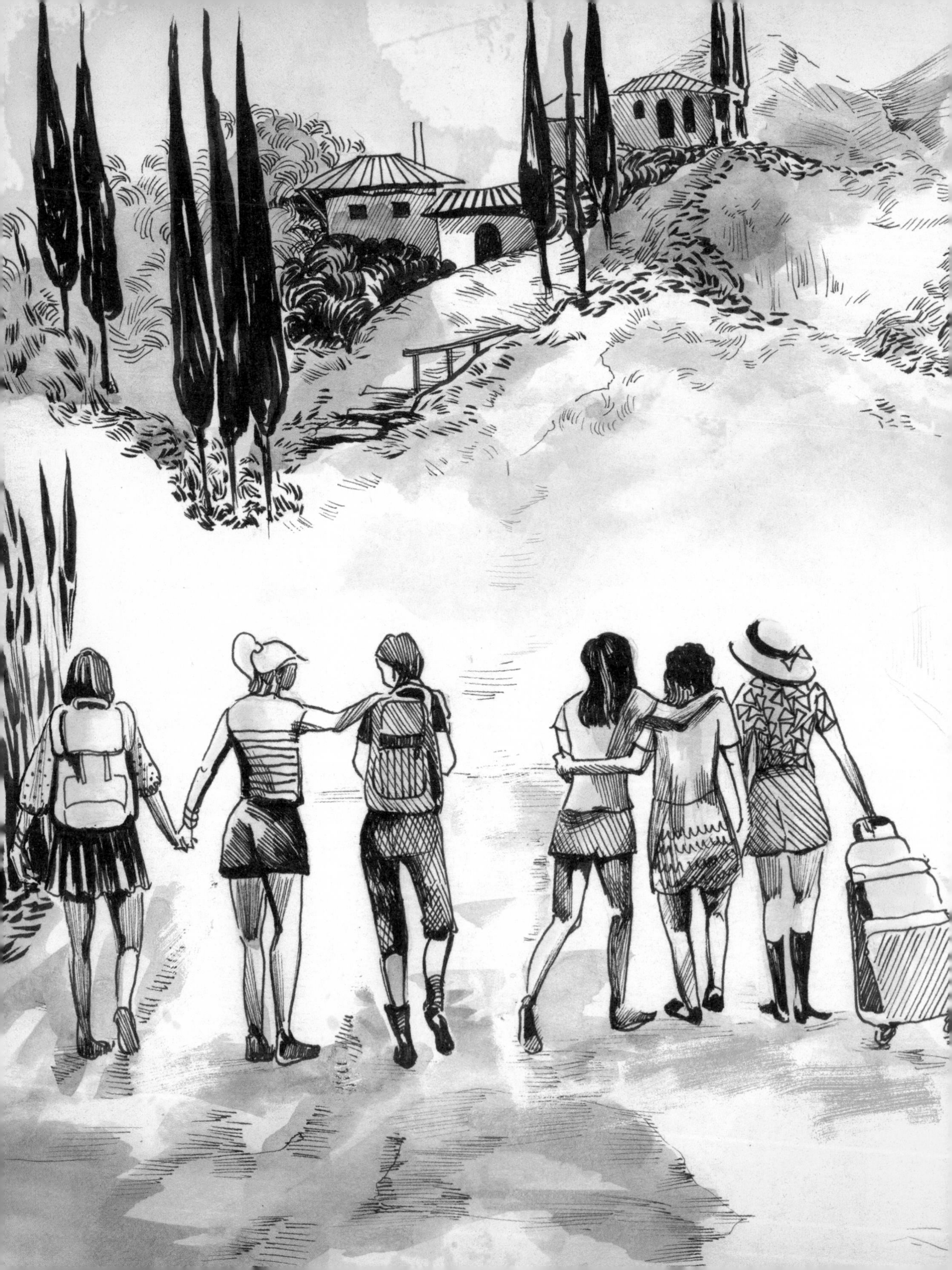

Some of them told me their own stories, a little like we are doing now. Two very nice girls from France invited me to travel with them for safety, because it is good for girls to stick together.

So, I did. I did not have any more trouble because I was extra careful after that and I traveled with partners I could trust. And I learned to speak some French! We were *fortes jeunes femmes unis.* (Strong young women, together!)

We all practiced saying *fortes jeunes femmes unis*, so now I know some French.

Also, "oui!" means "yes" and "non!" means "no," and both Joyce and Kaffers knew a "Yes" and "No" cheer that they taught us and we practiced it in English and with the French words:

Yes means yes, and
No means no.
Whatever I wear
And wherever I go!

Oui means oui, and
Non means non.
Whatever I wear,
And wherever I go!

I liked being able to say that in French, and I liked thinking about how I could travel safely if I joined together with *fortes jeunes femmes unis*, or even nice boys I knew well who were not strangers.

Then, it was time for my Joyce to tell her story.

I already knew a lot of her stories and secrets, like the time her baby brother sneaked into the kitchen and covered himself with peanut butter when she was babysitting him.

She had to hose him off outside before her parents found out, and they almost got caught when her mom asked who ate all the peanut butter.

But Joyce had a new story for me:

JOYCE'S STORY

This is a story you don't know about me, from a time before I was married to Harvey and came to live here.

I used to live in a very bad neighborhood, so bad that if you called a taxi to your house, they would not come because the drivers were afraid of being robbed.

I lived there because I did not have a lot of money. Most of the people were okay, but I still had to be careful.

I tried to talk a taxi into coming to get me when I was going to take a midnight train to Boston, to visit my sister Sybil. But I could not get anyone to show up.

I was taking the midnight train because it was way cheaper than the regular trains, especially if you bought your ticket in advance.

None of my friends had cars and there was no bus, so my only way to get there was to walk the long way down Market Street, at close to midnight and past all the closed and empty buildings.

I had two heavy suitcases, one in each hand, and I started to walk down that long dark sidewalk by myself. I stepped over the broken bottles and the garbage and kept my eyes wide open, looking out for trouble. And that's when I saw him.

A man stepped out of the shadows and started to walk towards me. He was not a wobbly drunk, like some of the men from around my neighborhood. Oh, no . . .

The alarm bell in my tummy went off. We all know what that means. He was walking straight at me. He was saying ugly things and telling me to come with him.

I was frightened. Both my hands were full, each holding a suitcase. If I thought he really wanted to just rob me, I could have dropped them, let him have my clothes and stuff. You can always get more stuff.

But you also know why I can't run very fast. You've seen the x-rays of my twisty bones, Dani.

I am built just a little too crooked to be a championship runner, like you. I was sure if he chased me, I would lose.

He had something shiny in one of his hands. I thought it could be a knife. He was talking angry sex stuff and moving closer and closer, but always in the shadows.

I made a decision. I walked sideways, just like a crab and right into the street, which was now the place where cars came off the highway that was up above, on an overpass.

The street had lights and I decided to keep walking down the middle of the highway-turned-street because the middle had the most light.

I went straight down the yellow line, trying to look determined and fierce.

Yes, that was dangerous. Cars were coming down the highway, even at that time of night. But I decided that I was safer because drivers were not out to hurt me and he was.

Also, I was following my own personal safety rule that I want you to learn now and remember:

If you are in danger, do not be afraid to draw attention to yourself, even if what you are doing seems like it is against the law or would get you in trouble.

You already know about yelling. You did a great job when you were in trouble at the park.

Other times, if you have to, throw a brick at a car or store window and set off their burglary alarm. Knock things over if you are being dragged. Yell and yell and don't care what anyone else would think. Whatever you have to do can all be explained later.

Or, in my case, jaywalk down the middle of the street because you know that angry and startled drivers will honk their horns, screech their tires and roll down their windows and yell.

I knew all that noise would be good. Guys like him don't want attention. They want things sneaky and quiet.

A second personal safety rule is this: *

Sometimes the safest thing you can do next is something that is *also* dangerous. But, it might be a danger you know you have a chance at handling.

I knew I could get hit by a car. But I also knew that if the cars kept making noise, it might bring the police.

The guy I was afraid of would probably not try to come out into the traffic, where there was light and people who might see him.

---

* What are your own safety rules? Do you have any family courage stories to tell?

Sure enough, a car came along, driven by two ordinary looking men. It was an ordinary car, driving very slowly, and one of them held out a shiny gold police-looking badge and told me to get in. They would take me the rest of the way to the station.

I did not get in their car. I was following another personal safety rule:

Be 100% sure *who* people who offer help are and if they can be trusted.

I thought to myself, "This is not an official police car. And anyone can buy a fake gold policeman's badge at a costume shop. What if these are two more bad men? I would never get into a car with strange men I do not know."

So, I said to them "Thank you for coming by. There was a guy in the shadows of that building who was threatening me. I see he has run away.

"I don't want to get into a car with two strange men. If you are police officers, you'll understand why. Could you, instead, please just follow me in your car while I walk the rest of the way to the station, on the sidewalk and not in the street?"

That was fine with them and, in a few minutes I saw a lady police officer walking towards me from the train station and she had a walkie-talkie. (This was before cell phones, in the Dark Ages!)

I saw that one of the guys was talking into a microphone in his hand and realized he had called on ahead for her to meet me.

The two guys were the real deal, plainclothes policemen in a plain car, disguised so they can watch troubled neighborhoods and sneak up on bad guys like the guy bothering me!

I walked up to them and said thank you, and that I was not sure at first if they were really police. They said that was fine and they were glad I was "using caution," which means being careful and protecting myself.

I asked them to give me their names and badge numbers because I wanted to write them a thank you letter and send a copy to their boss. (And I did! It is good to thank people, even when they are just doing their job, which is what they said.)

Then they told me I had better not miss my train and, even though I did not think I needed it, the woman police officer would walk me right up my platform and see that I got on safe.

We did that, and she said it was very good to meet a woman who was able to think fast and get herself out of a bad situation.

I said she could tell anyone else about my trick of drawing attention to myself so the bad guy would worry he might be seen and maybe get caught if he kept after me.

And she said that was a good trick. So I am passing it on to you, Danielle!

Joyce made her hands look like she was handing me an invisible present and I pretended to open it and put her trick in my pocket. It's a good idea to have and remember.

Then we hugged and Joyce did her pretend actress voice again and announced very loudly, "Last, but not least, we present the amazing Kaffers who, like all women everywhere, also has something to say about courage!"

Kaffers turned all pink in her cheeks because, even though she is a grownup, she can still get embarrassed by a lot of attention.

We all clapped and she took her seat and began our last story:

KAFFER'S STORY

"First, I want to say how proud I am to be here with you, Danielle, on this special day. I am very sorry about what happened to you. You did not cause that trouble. It was not fair. But, here we all are today, to celebrate your courage and honesty.

"Nothing bad happened to me in my story, unless you count when ignorant people said mean things to me, and you know what I think about that . . ."

Kaffers crossed her eyes and stuck her tongue out and blew a loud, wet and very rude noise that made me laugh. "In the end, a lot of those ignoramuses changed their minds and said they were sorry. Not everyone. There will always be some idiots who never learn and never change. Just ignore them. You know the truth even if they don't."

Then she started her story:

My story happened when I was a young adult who worked as a volunteer at our church. Most of the time I helped with our food pantry, packing up bags for hungry families.

I was also a substitute Sunday school teacher, if any of the other teachers got sick. Another one of my jobs was to help write and print the church newspaper.

That afternoon, I needed to get more paper before printing up next month's edition. Usually we had enough in the office closet but someone had used the last package, so I had to go down to the little storeroom in our basement, where we kept things like toilet paper and cleaning supplies.

I was in the basement, picking out the paper I would need, when I heard a very small noise, as if a little puppy had whimpered. Had someone left a dog in here for some reason?

It did not seem likely but I looked anyway and there, under the old sink that no longer worked, all pressed up against a corner, was little Francis Barrett, the boy everyone called Frankie B for short because we had two other boys named Francis in Sunday School and even a girl named Frances!

Frankie B looked as sad and as scared as I had ever seen any little boy look. He was shaking hard and pushing his fist in his mouth to keep from crying.

Back then, the kids all called me Miss Kathy and, when I bent all the way down and crawled towards him, the first thing he said was

"Please Miss Kathy, please go away. I want to be good. I do not want to go to Hell."

I told him that I was certain that little kids never went to Hell and probably most grownups don't either, but he kept shaking his head no. I managed to wrap my arms around him and he started to cry and cry.

It took me a long time to get him to tell me his story and it was an awful and confusing story.

What I found out was that one of our priests had been giving little Frankie "special private religious classes" all alone and by himself.

Only these classes had nothing to do with religion. Father Ronald was a sexual predator who hurt those little boys sexually and made them keep it a secret.

He lied to them and told them that, if they told anyone, they would go to Hell and so would anyone they told: their parents or even other priests. Then it would be all the boys' fault if those people suffered for eternity in the flames of Hell.

Frankie B was terrified.

Father Ronald's "special classes" with Frankie were just like the "secret games" Mrs. Kent's uncle forced her to play and his lies were the same kind of lies, all about hurting someone else if he told.

Only, this time Frankie was sure he had to believe Father Ronald because he was a priest and didn't that mean God was on his side?

Just then, I heard a quiet man's voice say,

"My poor child. God is never on the side of hurting kids and neither am I. Please let me help."

Standing in the doorway was young Father Luke, the priest who coached the boys' and girls' volleyball team and the one who wrote an entirely different (and much more interesting) Christmas Pageant for the kids to act out, with Joseph and Mary as two homeless people trying to find a hospital that would take Mary in because they had no money for health insurance.

Some people in our church thought Father Luke's ideas were too "progressive," that boys and girls should play in their own leagues: boys with boys and girls with girls.

They also hated the new Christmas Pageant, especially because Father Luke played an electric guitar and drums with the kids, instead of having old Mrs. McMurray at the piano, like always.

Young Father Luke had come down to the closet to get something he needed and had heard the whole thing. He bent down and started to ask Frankie B some questions, very gently.

Frankie B was very scared that day, but we took him home to his parents and we both told them what happened and helped him tell his story. Father Luke said it would be important for Frankie to go see a doctor at once.

At first, Mr. and Mrs. B did not want to believe that anything like this had happened to their son, especially to a boy.

Father Luke said it did not matter that Father Ronald was a priest or that Frankie was a boy. Father Ronald was the one who had committed a sinful crime and Frankie B was an innocent victim.

Father Luke said he was going to go back to the church and pray. Then he was going to take care of business.

After he left, I went with Frankie and his mother to see his doctor. I did not go to work at the church the next day because Tuesday was my day off.

On Wednesday, I went to see Father Luke first, and was very surprised and angry to hear that he had been "removed from his duties." That meant he was sort of fired from working at our church and no one would tell me where he was.

When I went to my own job, I was told that I was sort of fired, too. They would still pay me my weekly check, but I was asked not to come back until "the matter was settled."

Everyone was trying to act as if nothing had happened, except to kind of punish me and Father Luke for finding out the truth about Father Ronald. And Father Ronald was "away" too, everyone was told, although no one seemed to know where or why.

I told people what I knew, and that's when a lot of people I thought were my friends turned very nasty and even said I was spreading lies.

Well, I am happy to say that Frankie B's doctor did something like a Peter Pan paper shadow body drawing and some other things that helped him write a report that was sent to the police.

Soon after, a lady police officer came and talked to me and asked me a lot of questions. She said that she had already talked to Frankie B and was going to find Father Luke to talk to him.

I said I did not know where he went, but she said that she would be able to find him and Father Ronald and the other kids this had happened to because like you, Danielle, little Frankie B had given his own crime fighters some very good clues.

Mr. and Mrs. B and Frankie never came back to our church.

I went one more time, but mean Mrs. McMurray (who never got over being told her piano playing was not right for the Christmas Pageant) was telling everyone ugly things about me and Father Luke and making up awful stuff about the whole B family.

It was none of her business and she didn't know anything, anyway, but she blabbed her nasty stories to a lot of people, and I decided . . .

To *HELL* with them all!

When Kaffers said that, she had her angry face on, the one she used when she caught her son Ben and another boy fighting with sharp sticks that could really hurt.

No. Kaffers was angrier than that. She was the angriest I had ever seen her and now she had some of her Kaffers Waterworks Tears in her eyes. These were sad and angry tears.

She wiped them away with her napkin and kept going.

Two months later, I got a letter from Father Luke. He told me that he had found out from another priest that Father Ronald had hurt little boys before at another church. When he was caught, they just "talked to him" and sent him to another part of the country, this time to our church.

Worst of all, Father Luke knew that Father Ronald was now at another church, in another state, and Father Luke was in big trouble for warning people at that new church about Father Ronald being a sexual predator.

Father Luke said that I would be seeing him again soon, and not to worry. He said he knew that someone from the church offered the B family some church money to "help" Frankie "forget" what happened, and that made Mr. B so mad that he almost punched the money person out!

When I quit our church, I told them to stop sending me my "monthly check." Then, the same money guy who talked to the B family about paying to keep Frankie quiet, offered me a bunch of money in cash if I would forgive Father Ronald and then "exercise discretion."

I knew what forgiveness meant but I asked Kaffers what the rest meant, although I was starting to get the idea.

She told me that "discretion" was usually a good thing, it meant be extra careful about what you say or do, but this time she was being asked to "Shut up and pretend nothing had ever happened and maybe even LIE!"

When the rest of my Courage Party ladies heard that, they each said some angry things, even using bad language we do not need to include in this book (says Joyce).

The baddest words came out of Reverend Peggy's mouth, believe it or not, which kind of shocked me at first. Then I remembered how she could switch back and forth between regular and dictionary words and that seemed okay because she was seriously angry.

Reverend Peggy said this was a problem shared by many different churches, temples, mosques, and "other religious societies" (which meant Unitarians like her or Quakers) and even more groups I don't remember, all over the world.

She said many people only want to believe what they feel comfortable believing, and not that a sexual predator could use a house of worship as a way to disguise what they were doing and be a "wolf in sheep's clothing."

The picture of a wolf, disguised as a big sheep, leading a lot of little sheep or lambs into danger got into my head.

The boy who hurt me was a wolf like that. But there are also good kids who act like good big brothers, who are safe people. And Father Luke sounded like a good priest, too. Not a wolf.

Kaffers kept going with her story.

The next time I saw Father Luke was in a courtroom. He was not dressed like a priest then. Instead of a collar, he was wearing a necktie and he had on a sweater.

Father Luke was there to tell the truth about what he heard Frankie B say and so was I. Other people in the room included the B family, but not Frankie who was in a special room for kids with his advocate and his grandma.

There were other priests there and a lot of lawyers with them. There was no Father Ronald. They said he was in a hospital and too sick to come.

I looked at the judge and hoped he was smart enough to see that was probably a lie. Then the prosecutor for Frankie B and his family and some of the church lawyers for the defense went up to the judge and there was a lot of whispering.

I could not hear what they were saying and neither could anyone else.

The lawyers went back to their own sides: Frankie's side and the Church's side, and they all whispered some more. Finally, everyone nodded yes and the judge said a decision had been made.

Afterwards, Father Luke came up to me and told me to call him just "Luke" for now because he was going to take a sort of vacation from being a priest and go work with orphan teenagers in Central America for a while.

He said he already knew most of what the decision was because there had been a lot of meetings between all the adults before anyone had even walked into the courtroom.

No one on our side wanted Frankie B to feel forced to come into the courtroom to tell his story because he was a very little boy, littler than you, Danielle, and still terribly mixed up and very sad and really scared of seeing any priests. And there would be a lot of them in the courtroom, staring at him.

The Church did not want Frankie to tell everything that happened with Father Ronald, because that would put them in some serious trouble.

If there was a big trial, it would be in all the news and everyone would know more about the way they moved Father Ronald from church to church, without real consequences.

Consequences can mean punishment, even jail. Consequences are what has to be done next, to change things for the better.

Right now, it was like the predator adult was being protected and the kids were being blamed or ignored. Or made to stay quiet.

So the judge made a decision: Both sides were going to have to compromise.

Both lawyers came to an agreement. In court, that's often called a "plea bargain."

In the regular world, a compromise is when both sides think it is easier to get *some* of what they each want instead of fighting all the way to the end in a way that could hurt people.

With that kind of fighting, you end up with one winner and one loser. Good compromises, on the other hand, mean no one feels like a total loser.

Sometimes it's okay not to fight to the end, as long as you get most of what you need from your part of the compromise. I think it was good for Frankie B to be able to compromise.

What was happening to Frankie B may have been kind of like what could have happened to little "Mia." He was still feeling unsafe and scared and mixed up. That can be overwhelming.

I was glad Frankie B did not feel forced to talk about anything he was not ready to talk about. His Rape Crisis Center advocate helped his family understand Frankie and together they all figured out the best compromise.

Here's what they decided:

Father Ronald could never work in a church again. He had to stay in a place far away, with very old priests, and work in their garden after he "got better" from the hospital, which would probably be next week.

"Just Luke" made a sour face when he said that, and you all can tell why. We knew Father Ronald was hiding in that hospital from what he did!

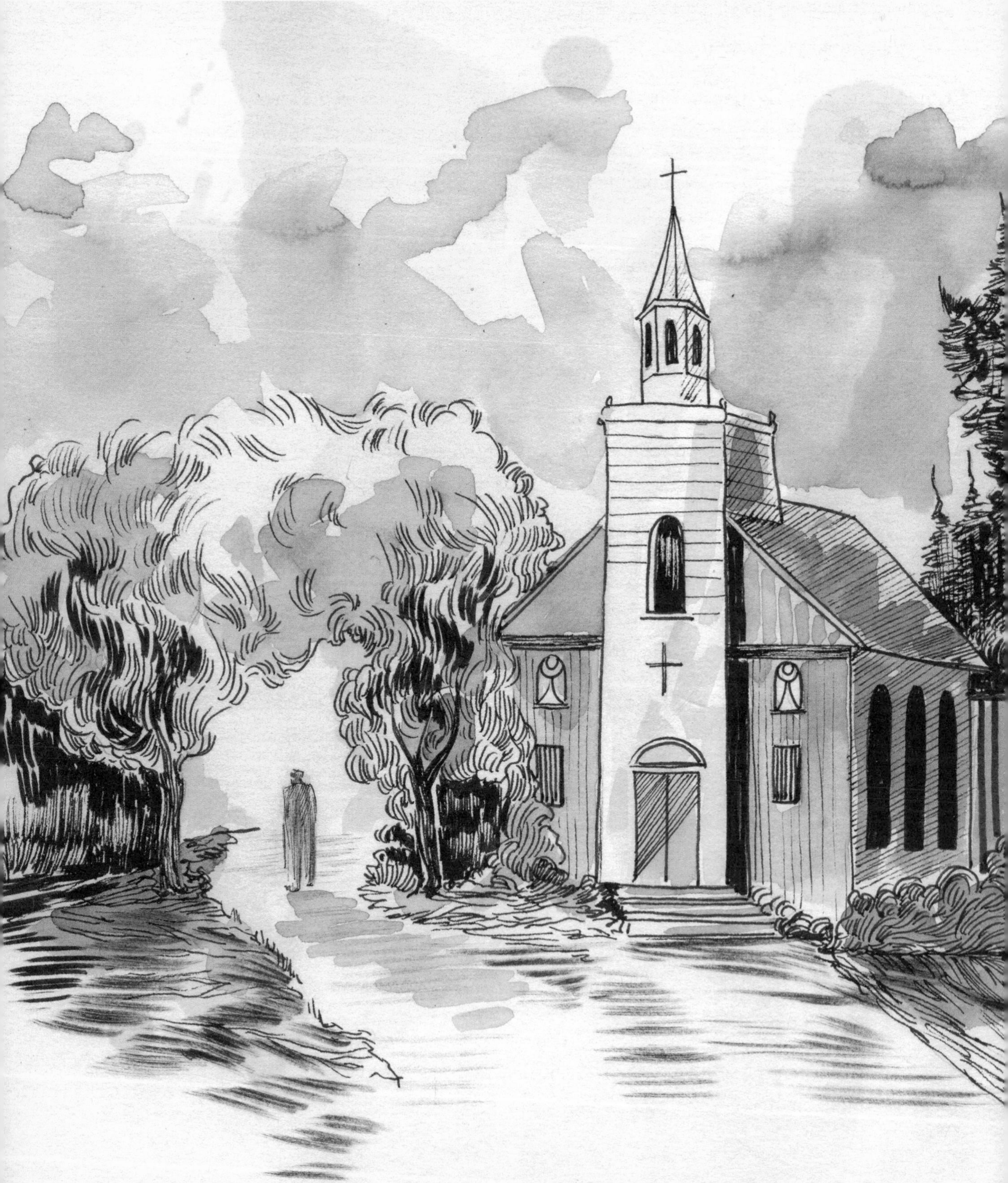

The lady police officer had given the judge a list of other children Father Ronald hurt, and now the Church had to give them money for help so they could feel better and safe.

Money could pay for a counselor or therapist for the kids and their families; a special summer camp for kids who survived violence; or for switching to another school in order to get away from all of the publicity or even other priests. Things like that.

The B family agreed not to talk to the newspapers but there had been a newspaper reporter in the courtroom the whole time, so whatever the reporter heard would go into the story, which was still a lot.

Reporters cannot be forced to shut up because America has freedom of the press and they can publish whatever they can prove is true.

I told Kaffers that Joyce showed me a tiny inch from our own newspaper about what happened to me in "a neighborhood park" and it never said my name or even the big boy's name, because we were both kids. If he had been a grownup, they would have used his name, but not mine, to protect my privacy.

Frankie B and his family would get money, too, but they would not be allowed to talk about how much, except to each other and to anyone he talked to for help, like his doctor.

That's what the Church did not want the newspapers to know. It was embarrassing to be spending money they raised to help people on a problem that they were responsible for stopping right away, but didn't.

I don't really know what else happened because I only talked to his family that last day, when they said thank you for helping Frankie.

Soon after, they moved away.

One more thing . . . A plea bargain can also mean that both sides came to an agreement without asking the judge to decide about right and wrong. And that's what happened.

I was kind of angry about this, because I really wanted it all out in the open and I wanted to see Father Ronald locked up in jail, instead of being given a nice little garden. He was a bad guy! Bad!

That's when Just Luke reminded me that the Church had a lot of money and, instead of using that to help the hurt kids now, they could drag the whole business out for years, while the kids would stay just stuck.

Just Luke also said he knew that no one from the Church would apologize to Frankie B for the awful thing that happened to him, so he was going to put on his priest clothes one more time that night, to go over and apologize for them.

Just Luke wanted to make absolutely sure that little Frankie understood that he did not do anything wrong and that everything Father Ronald told him about going to Hell was just a big lie he made up to trick him and the other kids he hurt.

Soon after this all happened, I went away to college. That Christmas, I got a card from Just Luke in Nicaragua that included a picture of him at his new job.

He was wearing a colorful shirt and he was smiling. He and his kids were practicing a Christmas pageant and he had his guitar.

Just Luke's letter said that the big Christmastime celebration kids have down there in Central America was in January, to celebrate when the Three Kings finally made it to where Baby Jesus was born.

January 6 was really when the first Christmas gifts were given, the frankincense, myrrh, and gold the Three Kings (or Wise Men) brought with them.

Just like he did for our kids, Just Luke wrote an updated version for their Christmas pageant. He had the Three Kings bring modern presents that all his kids decided the baby in the manger would have wanted to share with the world.

They brought Courage, Truth, and Justice.

Before coming here to this party, I looked on the Internet, to see if I could find out what happened to Frankie B. He went to college, where he learned ways to help kids who had been victims of sexual predators.

Now he is Frank B and he sometimes works with Rape Crisis Centers.

He also goes on speaking tours and tells kids, parents and anyone else who will listen all about what happened to him as a kid, that it happens not only to girls, but to boys and other kids, too and what he thinks we need to do to protect all kids.

Once he even talked to Congress about what should be done to keep children safe against Internet predators: adults who pretend to be kids so they can trick real kids into meeting them for sex.

Frankie B is not the same scared little boy I found hiding in his church basement.

After Kaffers told her story, Joyce had all my lady friends hold hands in a circle with me in the middle.

Everyone told me again how proud they were of my truthfulness and courage and how they would come to court with me, wearing business clothes and carrying briefcases, because that was how to show we were all serious and taking care of business.

Then we packed up the food and I went home and wondered what I would put in a serious person's briefcase, if I had one to take with me.

PART THREE:

HOW MY TRUTH AND COURAGE MADE THINGS BETTER

Okay, I know now that you'll think that all the help I got from so many good grownups and me wearing a Wizard of Oz courage medal would have made the next part easy but no, it was not. While we were waiting to go to court, bad memories still kept sneaking into my head.

Sometimes that happened when I was asleep and those were nightmares. Sometimes I just didn't want to do anything except sit and look at the floor and remember what happened and think why? Why do predators hurt kids? Why did this happen to me? Why did I go with him?

And sometimes I worried about what it would be like to go to court, where I would see that boy again. What would he say? What would I say? Would his mom be there to yell at me?

Joyce knew I was worrying about all this and told me we could always talk about it together but to remember, I had a whole team on my side and that I had some phone numbers to call if I ever thought I was having a hard time.

So, first I called Caitlin, my Rape Crisis Center advocate, and when we talked she reminded me of a lot of the things the other kids said in our kids group and what I learned about using my courage and telling the truth and how I wanted to keep our park safe for all of us kids, especially little ones too scared to tell what was hurting them.

Caitlin also reminded me that no matter what happened at court, I was already safe and had a whole team on my side, good grownups who would do the work of protecting other kids from that guy who sexually assaulted me.

Then she said we should just visit to chill and do something fun. She invited me to go with her and a bunch of kids to see a movie about a girl who was determined to save her little sister from bad guys on their planet.

First, the girl was the hero by herself and feeling alone. Then she got a lot of other kids and even some funny adults to help her.

In the end, it turned out she even helped save a whole lot of people she never even knew.

She had a cool bow and arrow and was smart and strong. There was a lot of fighting and smashing things and we kids all yelled and cheered for her team until the end, when the girl goes home to her mom with a boy who really liked her and had been helping her all the way.

It was good to be with kids who understood about going to court and stuff again. Caitlin is a good grownup and she gave me one of her helpful suggestions, which was something I did not have to do but might be a good idea to try.

Caitlin said it might be good if I also called and talked to Mr. Kovach, to let him know I was feeling anxious about going to court and having a trial.

I did not really want to call Mr. Kovach because I did not want him to think I was chickening out of being a champion Demon Wheeler. But Caitlin said she was making a *strong* suggestion, because she was sure I would feel better after. So the next day, that's what I did.

Mrs. Jenkins answered the phone and she was nice and cheerful and asked me how I was doing. I told her a little about my Courage Party and she said that's wonderful and was I calling for Mr. Kovach because he was right there and she knew he would want to talk to me.

I told Mr. Kovach more about the Courage Party and how all my lady friends were going to come to court wearing suits and carrying serious briefcases. That made him laugh and he said that was a great idea. We could never have enough serious briefcases.

Then he said there was now someone else coming to be on our team, an "unexpected assist" for us Demon Wheelers, who would really help.

I was confused and he apologized to me, explaining that he was using sports language because he was thinking about us winning our championship together, like he did with the other team.

An "unexpected assist" happens when someone does a sudden and unexpected thing, almost coming out of nowhere, to help put the team over the top or maybe even win.

I asked him who was helping us now with an unexpected assist, and Mr. Kovach said the word he should have used was "witness." Someone who saw something of what happened to me was ready to talk to the court and back me up.

I tried to think who this could be. I already knew about my policeman and his partner. I knew Dr. Anne was ready to talk about examining me and that she wrote a report. Was it someone from the family I ran past, when I was escaping?

"No," said Mr. Kovach. "This witness is even better. He saw the whole thing, except what happened to you when you disappeared into the woods.

"He saw you running away, being chased. He saw how that big boy wormed his way into a kids' game, got as close to you as he could by giving you a lot of special attention and then, how he sent everyone away to get soft drinks and snacks while he got you to go with him and how, soon after, you were running away from him, terrified and screaming."

I had to shut my eyes again, because this was making me see bad things all over again. I still did not know who he was talking about. Who was this witness? Mr. Kovach kept talking.

"All those boys playing basketball stuck together. Some of them knew that big kid from before and even looked up to him. Others thought he was a great guy for buying everyone snacks and acting like a coach.

"No one really wanted to stand up for the only girl on the team and some even acted jealous of all the attention he gave you.

"Others even seemed to think it was funny or did not understand what had happened. Still others had nothing to say to us or seemed frightened that the big boy might get back at them."

This all sounded like the same old "boys against the girls" thing that sometimes happened at school, unless we were all made to play mixed together and cheer for whoever does the best.

So, who was my secret witness?

"There was one boy who saw everything," went on Mr. Kovach.

"At first, his story was pretty much what we were hearing from the rest of the boys, all sticking together and not saying much. He was interviewed and we got his name. His mother was very unhappy about him being visited by a police officer and said so.

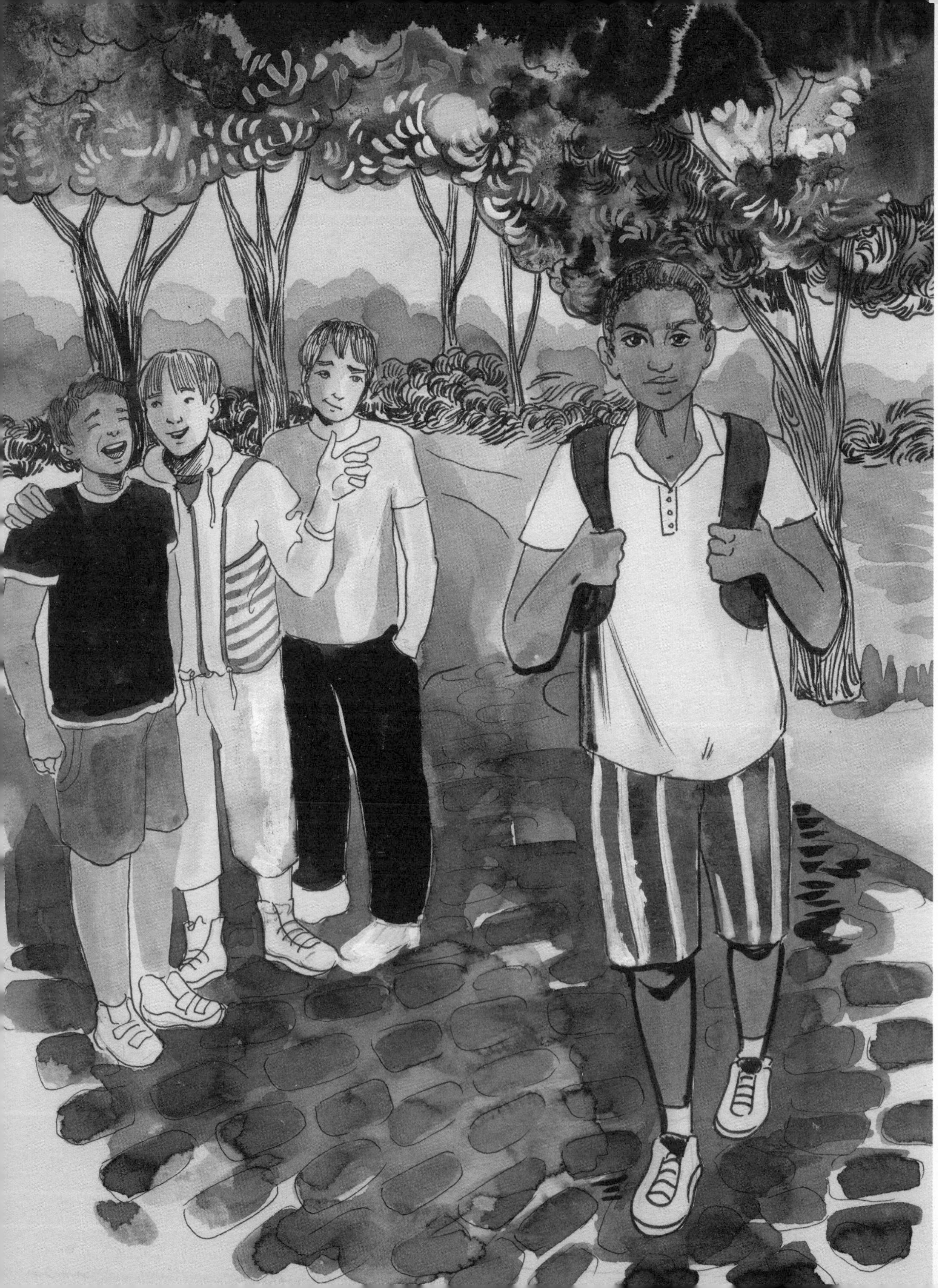

"But, something happened. She called us and said that not only had she changed her mind about cooperating with us, but that her son wanted to talk to the police again because he knew more than he first told them.

"She said he had been thinking about all kinds of things, especially about the kind of courage it takes to tell the truth and stand up against predators who would otherwise go on and hurt littler kids.

"He also said he was sorry to have first made fun of you and that he admired your courage medal.

"*Michael* is going to come to court when we do and, if he is asked, he will tell everything he saw and heard that day, no matter what those other boys say or do."

I was very surprised to hear this and I just stood there, saying nothing, while I thought about Michael and how he first laughed at me.

Then I said I guessed he had changed his mind and maybe, when this was all over, he should get his own courage medal or a Demon Wheeler button.

Mr. Kovach said that would be tricky until the case was finished because we did not want to make it look like we were bribing Michael and getting him to say what we wanted him to say by giving him a present.

I could understand that, but I was a little bit disappointed. I really thought Michael should get a button.

Mr. Kovach must have known what I was thinking when he heard that because he said that there would be nothing to stop me and Joyce from bringing the guest of my choice to sit in the front row of a Demon Wheelers game when the season began next Fall.

Then, of course, any guest of mine would get a complimentary Demon Wheelers button and maybe even a t-shirt if his team decided to make some for next season.

That sounded very good. We agreed that I should not try to talk to Michael until this was all over, although, if we saw each other at the pool, it was okay to be friendly and to stay there and swim.

Mr. Kovach said that "keeping a polite distance for now" was part of not bribing and not looking like I tried to get Michael to say what we wanted by being super friendly.

I could see his point.

The day we all went to court started out with me feeling all nervous, with my hands ice cold but holding on to my courage medal when I was not holding on to Joyce.

And, yes, my ladies were all there wearing lady suits, with skirts and jackets and carrying briefcases, even though I knew Dr. Anne usually just uses a big colorful patched cloth bag she got when she visited India.

Caitlin was there, too, wearing extra beautiful earrings and we talked some more about how it was going to be in court.

Then Mr. Kovach came up to us, using his crutches and wearing his legs and finally being taller than me. We were all lined up on a shiny wooden bench.

We heard, but did not see, the mother of the boy who hurt me. They were in a room nearby and their door kept opening and closing, so you couldn't tell much about what anyone in there was talking about.

She sounded like she did the day we drove up the hill to their house, all angry and loud and "My boy is a good boy and he didn't . . . !"

Mr. Kovach rolled his eyes and I asked him didn't she know he was in this kind of trouble before, with the little girl we called Mia and the "Dismissed with Prejudice?"

Mr. Kovach said she certainly did and she really wasn't helping her son by making all that noise or pretending he did not have a problem.

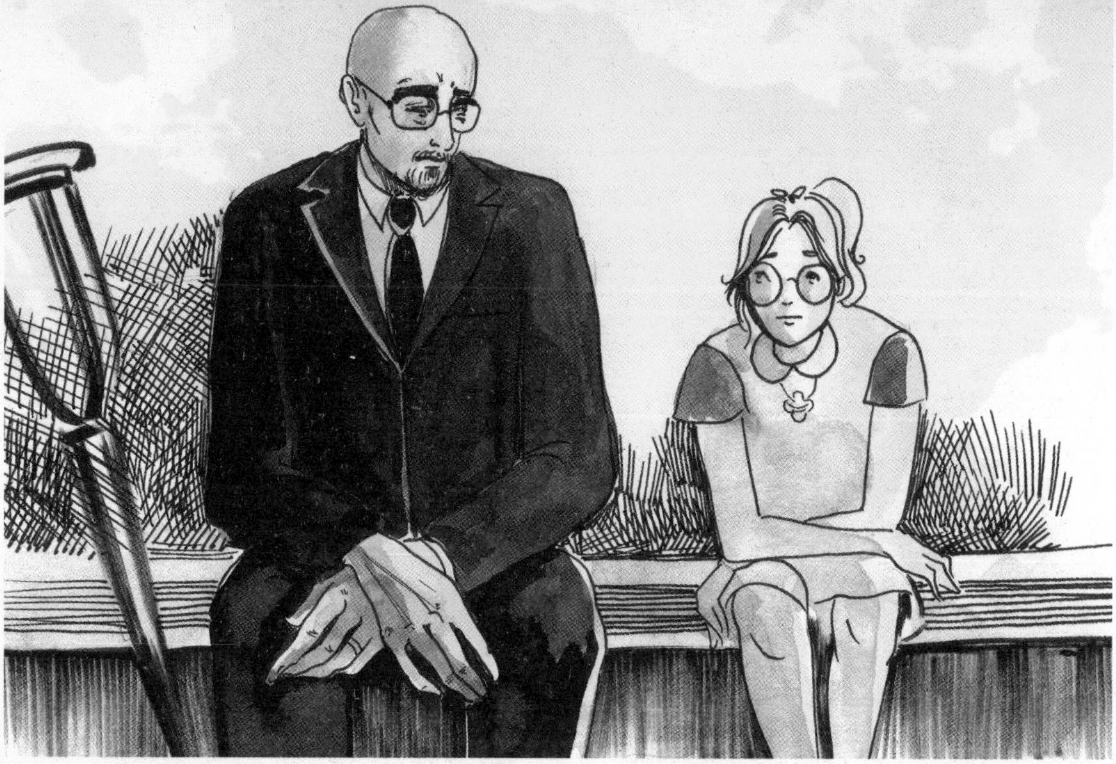

Then a person came over to talk to Mr. Kovach, who turned out to be the defense lawyer for the boy who hurt me.

The defense lawyer was a woman and she looked a lot like a school principal, serious but not angry unless you were in trouble.

She did not look at me at all. She came to get Mr. Kovach and they went around the corner to have a private conversation.

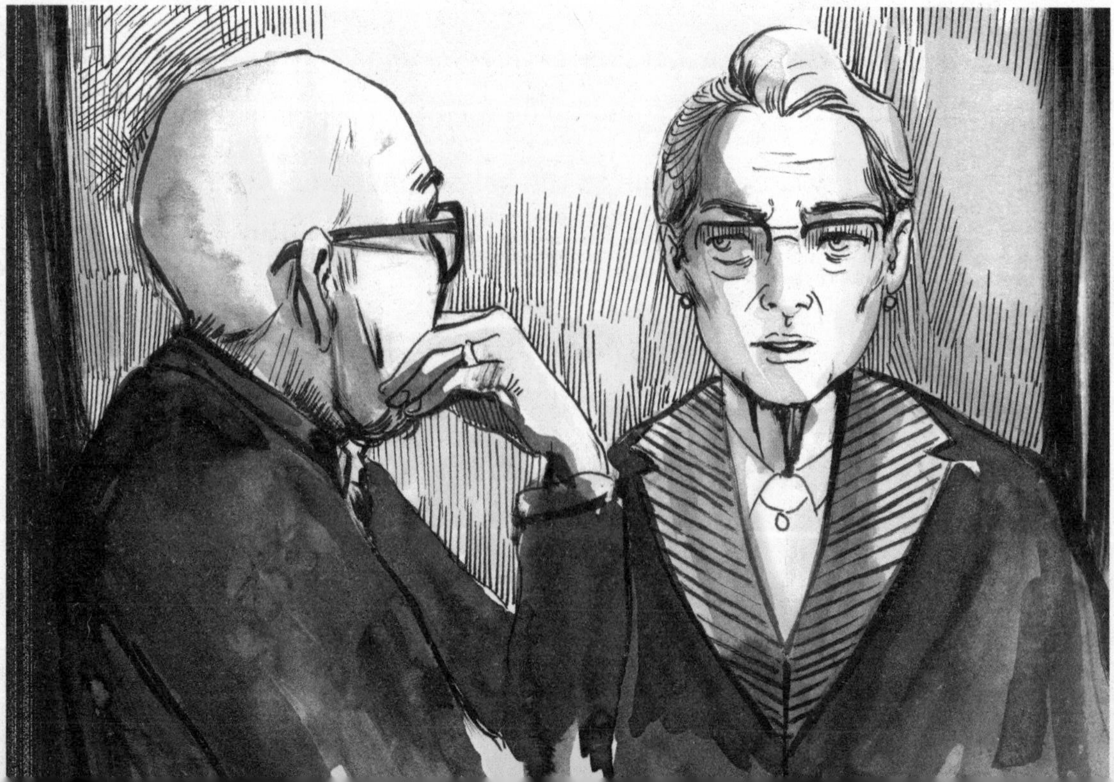

The boy and his family and his lawyer were the first to get called in to the courtroom by a court person whose job it was to come and get people.

Then, just before they got into the courtroom, I heard kind of a big fuss and then their defense lawyer came back to have another private conversation with my prosecutor lawyer Mr. Kovach.

They went somewhere else together and left us still waiting which was starting to make it all kind of boring and I started to count the tiles on the ceiling, although I was still nervous because we didn't think to bring me anything to do, like books or coloring, while we waited.

When Mr. Kovach came back, it was Joyce's turn to have a private conversation with him and the big kid's lawyer. Finally, it was time for Mr. Kovach and Joyce to tell me what was going on.

Mr. Kovach said that just before they walked into the courtroom where the judge would be sitting, the boy's mother had finally stopped shouting and made an agreement with her son's lawyer and with Mr. Kovach.

If I wanted, we could now have a plea bargain, (a compromise like what happened between Frankie B, the other boys and Father Ronald). Only there was not going to be any money being paid or sending the boy to a garden for the rest of his life.

Mr. Kovach said that the boy was going to sign a paper saying he attacked me and that way I did not have to go sit up next to the judge in front of people and answer questions because nothing had to be proven anymore. Everything could be taken care of now, instead of going on and on, back and forth.

The boy admitted what he did and he was going to be punished and the judge wanted Joyce and me to come into his office, which was in a little room behind the courtroom.

I asked why and Mr. Kovach said the judge wanted to talk to us about what kind of punishment for the boy and what else should be done to make things right for me.

I had been thinking so hard about what I would have to do or say in the courtroom that I had forgotten all about how the boy who hurt me would be punished, if he was found guilty. I did not know what to say.

When we were introduced to the judge, he was not wearing his big black robe. It was hanging on a coat hanger, on a hook behind his door. He was in shirt sleeves and he wore red suspenders. His desk had folders like the one Mr. Kovach showed me before.

One of them was that same folder that had the boy's name on it and now, a paper stapled on it that had my name and a lot of other words I could not really read, because they were sideways.

When you talk to a man judge or a woman judge, you are supposed to call them "Your Honor," which is something I learned before I went to court.

We sat down and he looked at some papers and then he looked at me and said he was very glad to meet me but sorry that it was because of what the boy did to me.

He was also glad to meet Joyce and said he would ask her first what kind of punishment should the boy get and did she think he should be locked up in a kind of jail for kids?

Joyce said that the first thing she wanted was called "no contact." That meant the boy would get arrested if he ever came anywhere near me.

She also wanted it so he could never go to our park again. I said I thought that sounded like a good idea to me, and the judge said he agreed and wrote something down.

I thought we should be over by now, but Joyce had more to say, like she does a lot of the time when we have school teacher parent conferences and she has lots of questions about how I am doing.

Joyce said she had worked in juvenile detention centers—the real word for kid jail—and in men's prisons for many years, before I was even born and that she thought a lot of times those places made mixed up and hurtful kids even more violent.

She also said she knew that many times people who sexually assaulted kids had learned to hurt that way from people who sexually assaulted them when *they* were kids.

We did not know the big boy's story and maybe he needed some good grownups to help as well as some punishment. Maybe he had been sexually abused and was copying what happened to him. In a juvenile detention center, he might get sexually abused by even bigger kids . . . Or he might just keep on abusing the littler kids. Joyce knew that happened a lot and for real.

I thought about some of the stories kids told me in our kids' club and could see how that could be true.

Joyce said she had been looking around and there was a place that tried to help kids who had committed crimes "of a sexual nature," like what he did to the other little girl, 'Mia,' before he went after me.

Joyce said that she wanted that boy to go there so people could find out why he was acting like that and then maybe he would get the help he needed to change and stop his predatory behavior.

The judge was a little bit surprised by that but he said yes to that, too, if it was okay with me, and it was.

After he wrote down what Joyce wanted, he looked at me and said very seriously, "Well, Danielle. This boy did a terrible thing and he hurt you. You have heard how Joyce wants him to be punished. I now need to hear from you, because you were the victim. How do you want him to be punished?"

I said I wasn't really a victim anymore because it was all over for me and really, I was just a crime fighter and I did not know what was supposed to happen after the telling the truth and having courage part.

The judge smiled when he heard that and then he said to tell him what kind of punishment did I think would be strong and serious and teach him a lesson to never do this kind of thing again.

I thought and thought about the worst punishments I could think of, like if I were to get in trouble at home.

Some kids get the belt, but living with Joyce means living in a no hitting house. When I do something wrong, I get "consequences."

I thought about this one time when I really got in trouble and decided the consequences I had then might be fair for the big boy now. I wasn't really sure if I was giving him the right answer, but I said

"Ummmm . . . Maybe take away his radio listening for two weeks, Your Honor?"

That's one of my worst consequences for bad behavior because I really love to hear the newest music, especially while I am getting dressed in the morning and I hated it when that was my punishment.

The judge looked at Joyce and they both smiled and nodded, like they understood and agreed about something adult.

Then the judge said he liked my thinking about all this and he was very happy to have met me.

He shook my hand and for a minute I wondered if I was supposed to bow or something.

But, there was Joyce pulling me next to her with a big squeeze and that is how we walked out of his office and back to all my people who were waiting for me all that time.

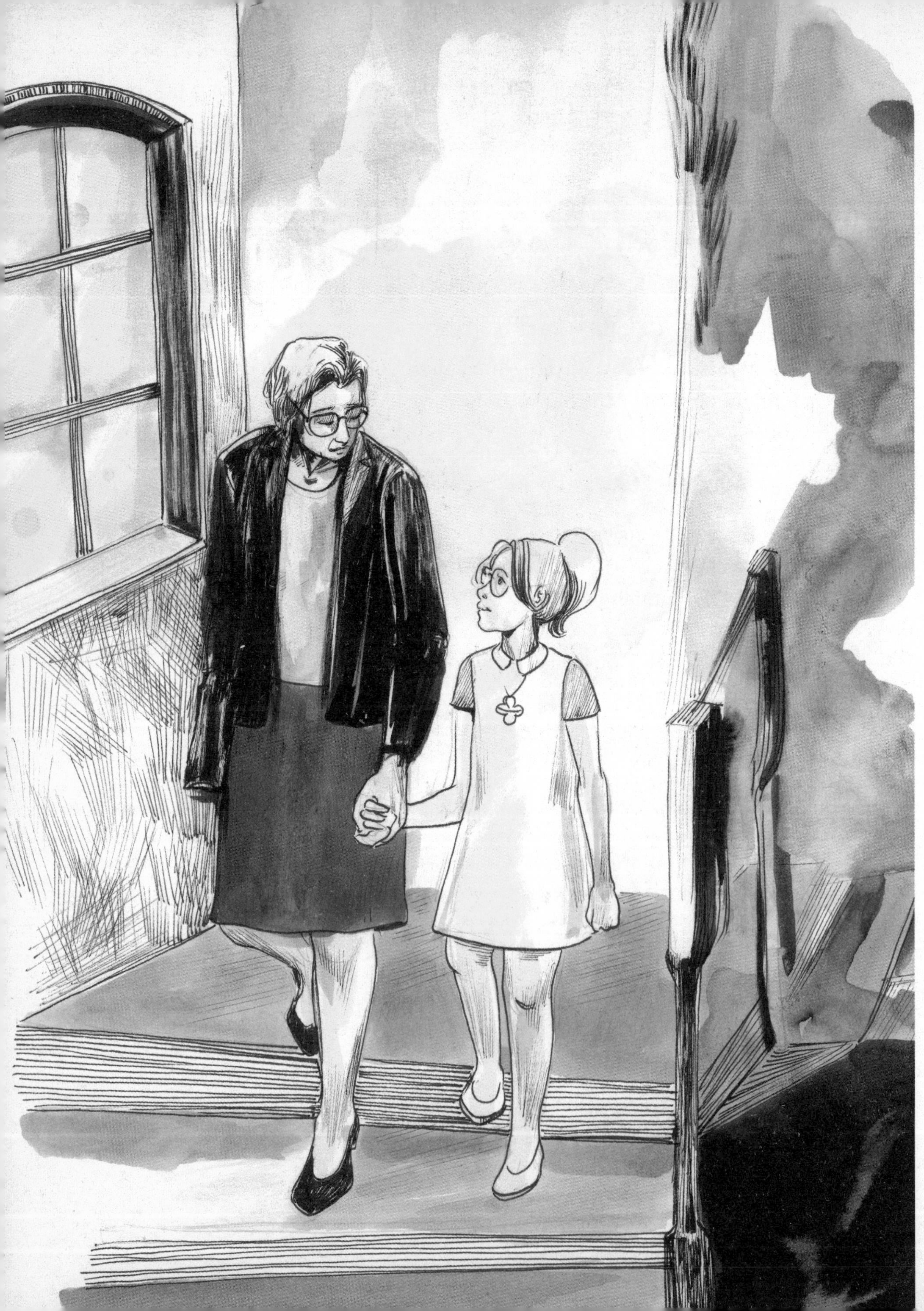

PART FOUR:
AFTER I USED MY TRUTH AND COURAGE

I have used my powers of truth and courage for other reasons since court, like if there is a problem at school or when I know someone is doing something mean to another kid, especially the littles.

I see Caitlin at the rec center where I take her self-defense class and we all practice kicking and shouting "No!" real loud.

Sometimes I see her bringing in a new kid and I wonder if they are there just to get stronger, or if something bad happened to them. I don't come up and ask them but I am always there to listen, because I know how it is.

When I think about it now, it's more like I was in some kind of car crash that was a long time ago. It was scary, and I got hurt but now there's nothing broken or bad except for sometimes bad memories that are getting easier to push out of my mind. These days, if I want to wear another kind of necklace, I put my courage medal around Blueberry Bear's neck, because he is part of what happened.

I like to wear it still when I have to try something hard, like being in a competition or on the first day of starting a new grade at school.

I go to the park now, but I try to stick with kids I know and I keep my eyes open.

Michael told me he took his little sister to meet my policeman at the City Hall Safety Fair for kids. She got a coloring book about Stranger Danger and even met Officer Bruin, so now she knows who to ask for help if she ever needs it.

Joyce and I took Michael to a Demon Wheelers game, where they did decide to have t-shirts for their friends and families to wear.

We both got one and Michael got his Demon Wheelers button. At first, he was amazed to see Mr. Kovach really did not have any legs, but soon he got used to it and was yelling, "Go! Go!"

I think the Demon Wheelers are going to be champions again this year because they are the best, better than those teams on TV.

We never heard from that boy again. People say his family moved away and I hope he figured out why he was hurting kids smaller than himself and learned how to stop it.

I know I want to be some kind of artist when I grow up, although I also want to help kids in trouble. Joyce says that of course I can do both.

I like how this book turned out, especially the drawings Gerta made. But, maybe instead of drawing books I'll draw on people and give them interesting tattoos. I could tattoo Joyce and Caitlin!

This part is really the end of the book and I hope you liked it or at least understood why some of it had to be a little sad or scary.

That's the way real life is, sometimes, but if you ever find yourself in the middle of something bad, now you know to use your courage and tell the truth. Find that one good grownup.

We don't always get rescued right away but whatever it is that is hurting you can and will end if you keep trying to get good help.

Because someone reading this might need help now, we are adding a special part at the end of this book with phone numbers and other information and good ideas.

Also, my Joyce is going to write something more for good grownups to read. You can read what she says because we have no secrets in this book.

Okay? I have to get to bed early because I am going to try out for our after school basketball team. I need my rest because I am still short and some of the kids in my class came back from summer vacation and I can see they are starting to grow real tall.

Wish me luck and I will wish you good luck, too.

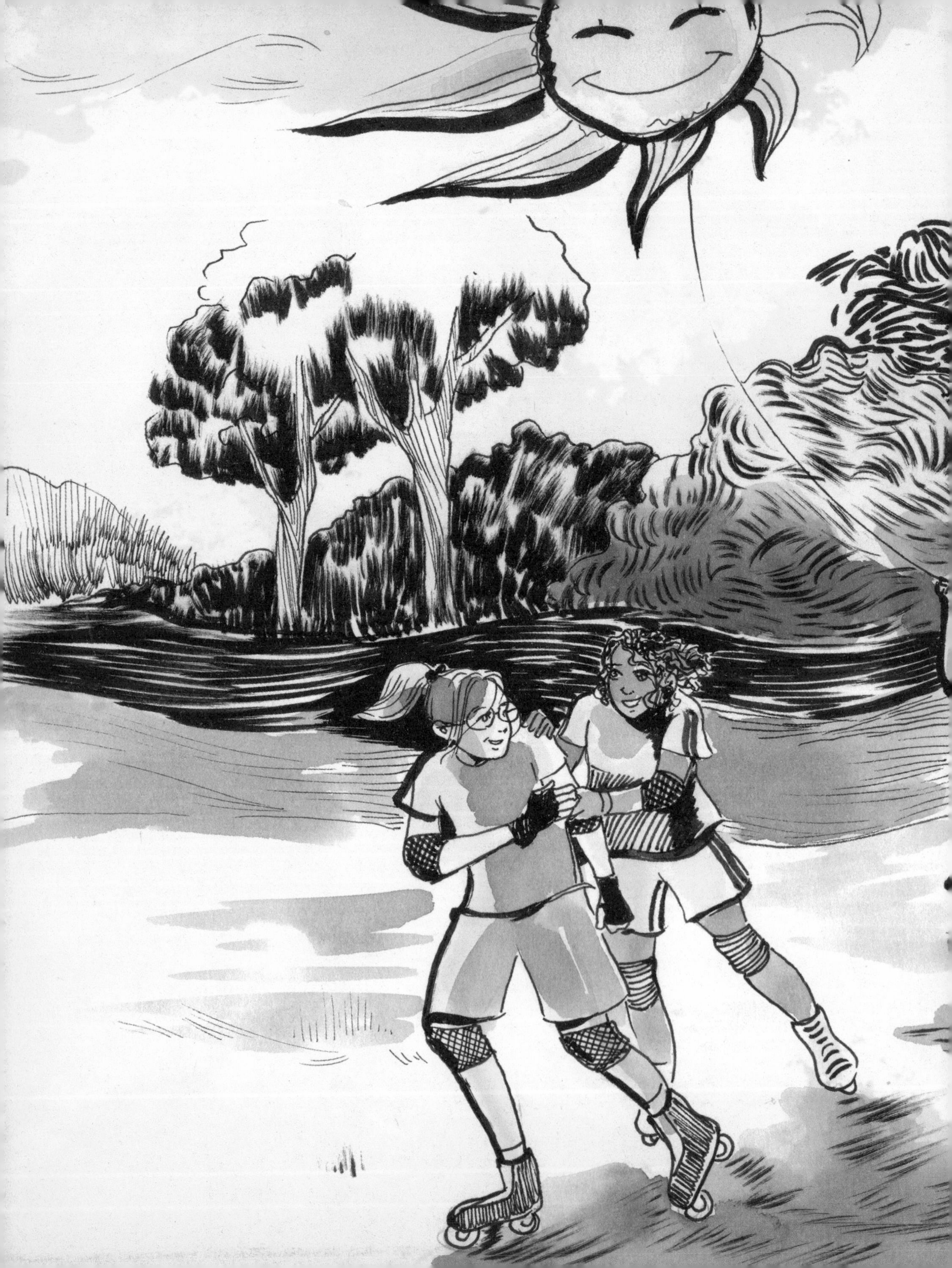

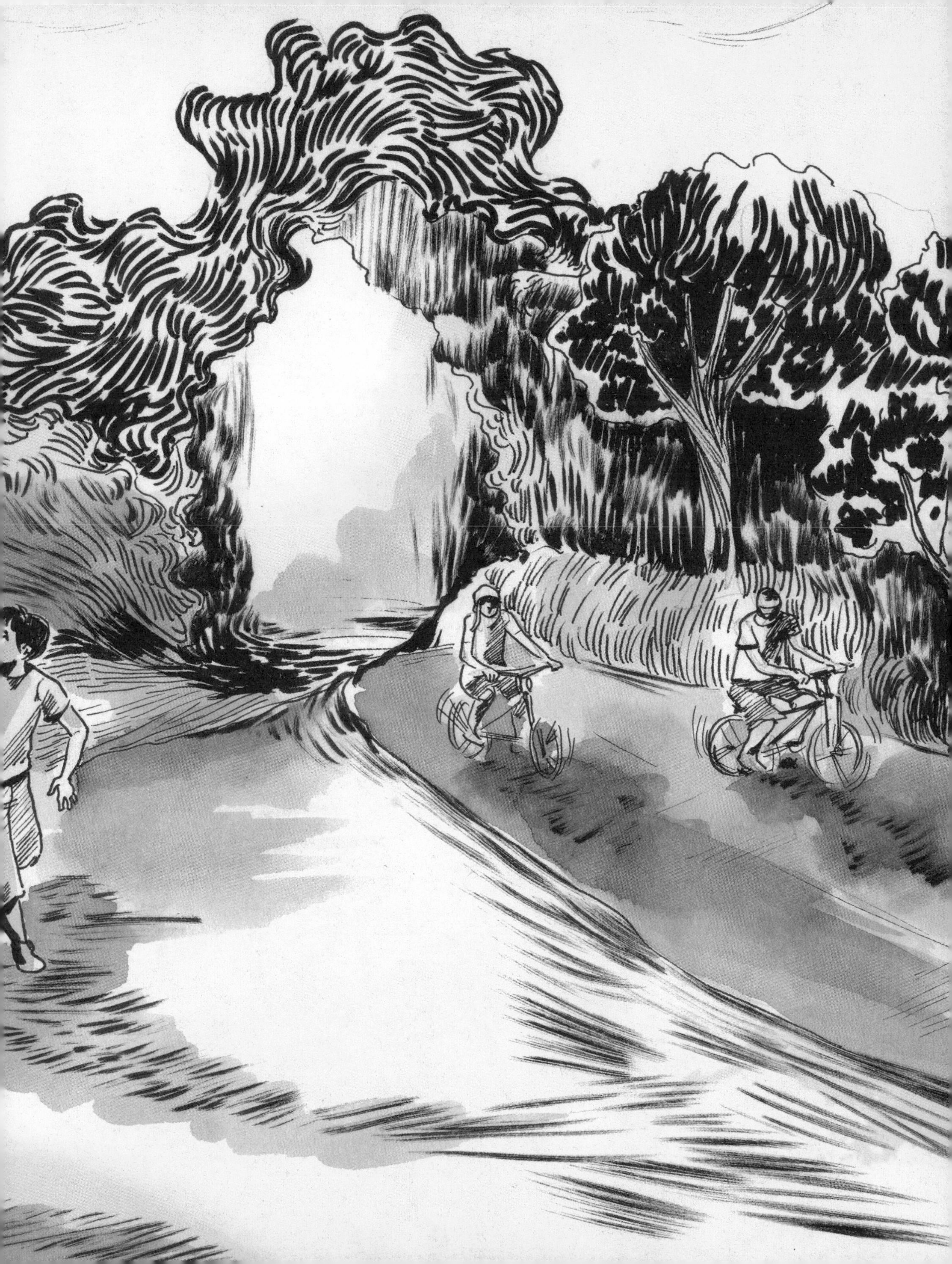

PART FIVE:
GETTING HELP WITH YOUR OWN TRUTH AND COURAGE

FOR GROWNUPS

There is no sound as terrible as the sound of your own child screaming for help. I could hear Danielle's voice even before she made it to our front porch and we met halfway inside the house, her sobbing as she ran up the stairs to find me and me racing down from the third floor, where I usually work.

It did not take me long to realize she had been sexually assaulted. It's possible that my reaction was a little bit faster than most because I have had some experience with this kind of trouble. What I remember thinking while she wrapped her arms around me, shaking and still not able to tell me exactly what happened, was this:

How Danielle sees me react, whatever I do next, is going to shape what she will feel, think or remember about this for the rest of her life.

I guess I saw the big picture. I tried to imagine what would come next, how I wanted her to feel in the next hour, the next week, five years from now, 10 years . . . as a young adult, and as a person my age.

And yes, we had already been through difficult times and family drama. There were painful reasons why she now lived with us as guardians, instead of with her biological parents.

No more drama, I kept thinking. De-escalate so we can both cope. Yes, it is terrible, but no drama!

My Danielle had already been through rough times. Every time we had hit a crisis before, my impulse was always to stabilize things (even when I was scared myself or just feeling rocked way too far off balance.)

I would not have the idea for a Courage Party until a day or so later, but my mind does work like that. I'm a creative problem solver who believes in the power of art, books, and storytelling.

I also knew how shame and guilt hurts survivors, often causing deeply pained and lasting changes in one's life, knocking you off track from the person you were becoming. No drama. No shame. No guilt.

I knew something else:

A crime had been committed, one that should have no more stigma than being robbed of a wallet at gunpoint. But stigma and shame are still part of our culture. My child was going to take her cue from me.

People would take their cues from her.

If we both were open and unashamed, if we decided how this story would be told, then it would become, when it was over, a wholly different kind of story.

I'm one of those people who tries to turn hurt into understanding and, as a writer, I understand best by turning rough times into stories.

I knew that someday Dani would be telling this awful thing in front of us now to someone else, as a story, although we did not think about making a book like this until years later.

Finally, I knew about the power of women's experience, women's wisdom. I knew where to find the help I would need to support and better prepare my child. Reminding myself of this sparked the idea of a ceremony or party. No, I didn't see this as a rite of passage. And I especially did not want Danielle to think everyone is a target. (But, stuff happens.)

What I tried to create for her was something more healing and strengthening than what would be offered by our too often flawed judicial system—even though I have been a part of that system and have seen how hard people inside that system often work to set things right. Danielle's police officer, advocate, attorney, and the judge who tried the case were kind, wise, and just.

I'm a feminist, someone who believes in full equality for all genders. I am terribly aware of how sexual assault targets everybody, regardless of gender, and that little boys, grown men, and people who don't identify as male or female are too often left out of the picture when we talk about sexual assault, abuse, or rape.

I make a brief appearance in a documentary about my late friend Barry Crimmins, *Call Me Lucky*. Barry used his own super powers of truth, courage—and searing humor—as he talked about his transformation from terrified, exploited child to the good grownup little Danielle grew up calling

"Barry Criminal, my friend the NOT criminal and child protector."

Find that film, look up his writings, and look out for anyone else speaking out for our little boys.

I would love to see parents having Courage Parties for their children rather than whispering their anger and anxiety to each other in their bedrooms because our children do hear us. We have to stop giving them conflicting messages.

When Danielle told the judge she thought her attacker should be punished by taking away his radio for two weeks, I knew she was going to be alright. She didn't want him locked up to protect her. She did not want him brutally punished. She didn't want revenge. Danielle only expected this, most likely, damaged other child to receive consequences (as she understood them) for "bad behavior."

In our own way, we had "normalized" something terrible. This didn't make it okay, but it kept trauma from digging in under her skin and developing like a life-destroying cancer.

Throughout the events of this book, Dani was given control appropriate to her age of her own story, of her own circumstances, with "good grownups" on all sides ready and able to help.

No matter how young a victim, it is important that they feel they own and control their own story. If they are just pinballs, bounced around in a confusing legal system, their pain does not end with a verdict.

All of our kids have the ability to tell the truth and react with courage. Dani is, of course, the best and bravest true-to-life superhero crime fighter I'll ever know but so are your kids.

So are all of our kids, whenever we put aside our self-interest and fears or shame and really listen. We can all be good grownups and maybe that starts when we are brave and truthful with each other, willing to help and ready to share what we know.

P.S. If you are one of those always curious kids who read this part I just wrote to help good grownups understand my ideas, you might want to talk to your own good grownup about what you read and about what kind of help you think good grownups can give.

You can also send us an email or letter, to let us know what is important to you. I'll let you know how you can reach us or other people who can help you understand more.

If you are a kid who is being hurt, here are some things to know and do that can really help:

FOR KIDS

We like to get letters and drawings but, if you or someone you know is in trouble, the *best* and fastest way to get good grownup help is by finding and telling a good grownup.

Just tell your good grownup out loud or in a note:

"I need your help. Can we talk about something serious?"

If it is hard to find a good grownup, here are some phone numbers to try. Your call will be answered by a good grownup advocate, like Caitlin, or a police officer (like the one who helped Danielle).

IF YOU HAVE BEEN HURT, OR IF YOU THINK SOMEONE IS GETTING READY TO HURT YOU…

DIAL 911 (Call the police)

If you're afraid to have a police officer come to your house, you can always ask them to meet you someplace safe. Or:

CALL YOUR CLOSEST RAPE CRISIS CENTER

LOOK UP THE NUMBER NOW AND WRITE IT DOWN HERE:

IF YOU DO NOT KNOW THAT NUMBER CALL:

National Sexual Assault Hotline

(800) 656-4673

ChildHelp

(800) 422-4453

If you can't use a phone, you can find an advocate to chat online with at

online.rainn.org

It's okay to be scared when you call. This is a good way to find grownups who can help.

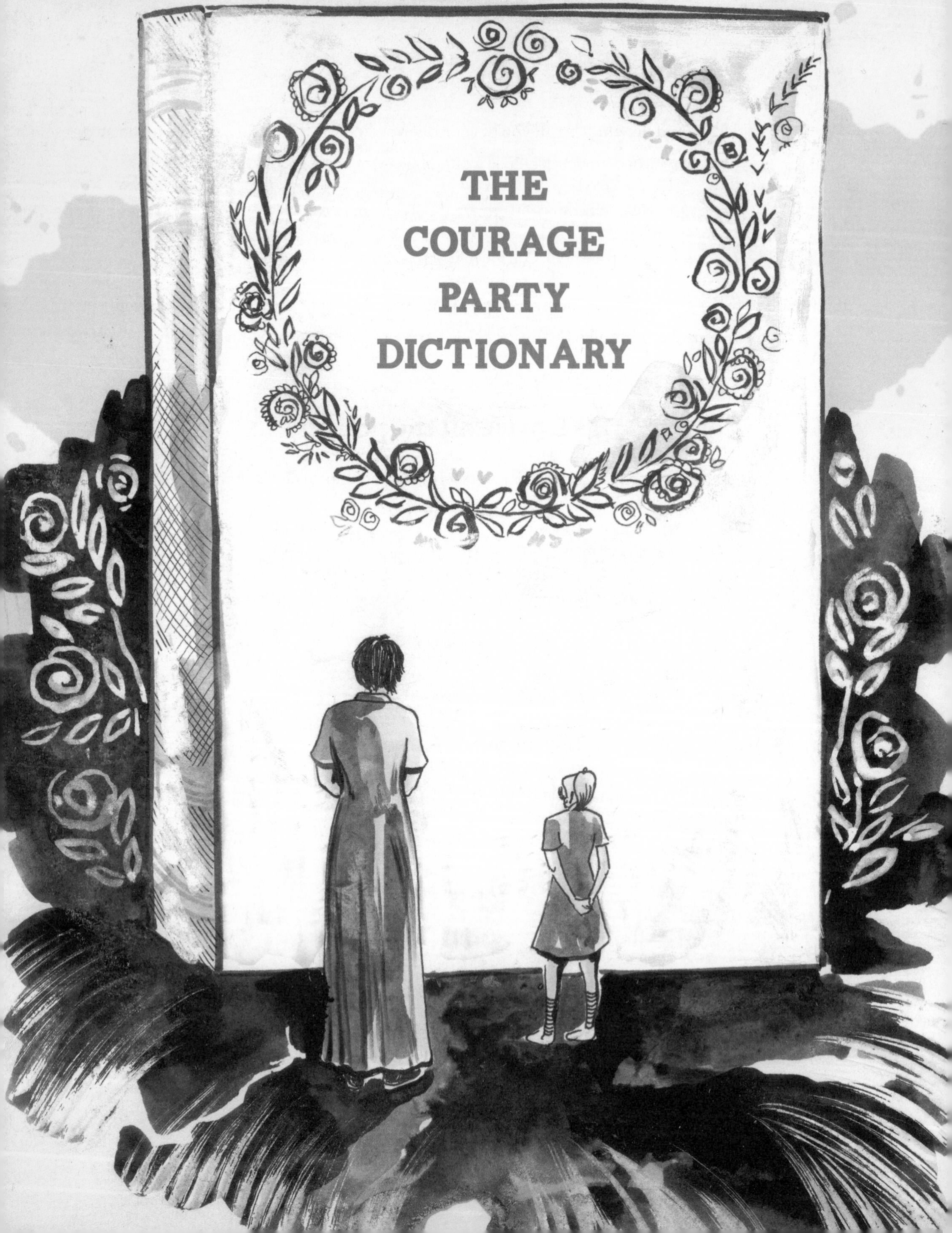
THE
COURAGE
PARTY
DICTIONARY

DANIELLE AND JOYCE'S DICTIONARY LIST OF WORDS USED IN THIS BOOK

BUTT OR BUTTHOLE: We think you know this one. Butt is short for "buttocks" and the scientific word for butthole is anus. Your anus is not the same as Uranus. Uranus is a planet.

GENITALS: Sensitive, special private parts of your body in between your legs and on your front side.

PENIS: Boy genitals.

VAGINA: Girl genitals.

SEXUAL: A word that means having to do with genitals.

SEXUAL INTERCOURSE: A way for two people to connect their genitals for adult loving enjoyment or to make babies.

CRIMINAL ASSAULT: To attack. To hurt. Anyone of any age can be criminally assaulted.

SEXUAL ASSAULT: Sexual attack. Sexual hurting. Not the same as loving sexual intercourse because an attack means force and overpowering. A criminal sexually attacks someone else's breasts, body, or genitals with their own genitals, hands, mouth, or anything else, including an object (a thing). Can be bad sexual touching, grabbing, or poking. Can be rape. Can be forced oral sex. Anyone of any age can be sexually assaulted by a criminal.

Sexual assault happens without permission. Kids cannot give permission to be sexually touched. It is a crime to sexually touch kids. Sometimes called sexual molestation.

SEXUAL MOLESTATION: Another word for sexual assault, like we just explained. Sometimes called sexual molesting.

RAPE: Legally, this is sexual assault involving penetration by any body part or object into genitals, mouths, or anuses, even a little bit. Anyone of any age can be raped by another person.

ORAL SEX: Mouth-on-genitals sexual touching.

Forced oral sex is sexual assault. Oral sex with permission between grownups is not. Kids cannot give permission for oral sex. It is a crime for someone to have oral sex with a kid.

SPERM: Little tiny guys that look like tadpoles under a microscope that can travel from a penis during sexual intercourse up through a vagina, to start a baby.

EGG: Not a chicken egg for breakfast. In humans, a tiny dot that makes its way every month into the vagina. If it welcomes the sperm during sexual intercourse, that can start a baby.

PERIOD: Also called menstruation. When a girl gets older, her body produces tiny dot eggs every month that sit inside her, waiting for sperm. Not every egg meets a sperm! Only a very few eggs ever join with sperm to make babies. Otherwise you would have a zillion brothers or sisters and the world would be terribly crowded. All the eggs that do not start babies stick around for a few days and then leave the body through the vagina, along with a little slippery blood.

Because that can be messy, most girls wear sanitary pads, tampons, or other pads to catch the blood and keep their under panties clean. Then they throw the pads away. Pads and baby diapers are made of the same stuff, so they soak up anything wet.

When a girl first finds blood between her legs or in her panties, she knows she has started having her period.

PUBIC HAIR: The hair that starts growing in between a kid's legs and in their armpits as they become older. At the same time, some people can start growing face and chest hair.

BREASTS: Really? Everyone has them. An adult's breasts are bigger than a child's breasts (though most people with flatter chests don't call them breasts and only call them chests). Some people don't like that they have prominent breasts and use a special piece of clothing called a binder to help make it look like they don't have any. Everyone's breasts start to change about the same time pubic hair shows up.

Some breasts are designed to feed babies. Most of the time, people dress them up in pretty clothes like bras, colored undershirts, or sports tank tops. Their breasts. Not the babies. Babies get other kinds of pretty clothes. We have never seen a baby wearing a bra.

You've got this.

HOW TO PLAN A COURAGE PARTY

Everybody's Courage Party should be different, because we are all different kinds of people who like different kinds of things. Get one good grown up (or more) to help with planning, invitations, and explaining.

Joyce found Danielle's Courage medal at a store that sold a Wizard of Oz bracelet. She took off the Cowardly Lion medal part and put it on a chain. But you can have any kind of medal, or special ring or anything else. Many pet stores have machines that make cat or dog tags that you can have engraved with a message. We like the round ones better than the ones that are shaped like dog bones. Or skip the whole medal thing and do something else.

We think you already know what kind of food you'll want and if you want to make a cape or even a crown to wear.

Danielle had an all-women Courage Party with all her good grown up lady friends. But you can invite any good people you like. Just be sure to make time to tell your own story and then listen to each other tell more stories. There is no one, perfect way to have a Courage Party.

If you want to draw a picture of your Courage Party and send it to us, that would be awesome. We think drawings are more fun and more private than photographs.

If you want to make your own comics or books about your own true tale of truth and courage, that would be absolutely amazing. We would like to see any comics, stories, or pictures you make.

We can be emailed at: couragepartybook@gmail.com

Regular stamped mail can be sent to:

The Courage Party
P.O. Box 18471
Cleveland Heights, OH 44118

HOW TO HELP KIDS GET PRINT COPIES OF THE COURAGE PARTY

You can get a free (low resolution) ebook to share at **CourageParty.com**, "The Courage Party Book" on Facebook, or by emailing **couragepartybook@gmail.com**

Help promote this book on social media. We will send e-copies to people who hear about us from you or anyone who asks.

• Please also send an encouraging word or two back to us at **couragepartybook@gmail. com**.

• Make a donation via PayPal to **couragepartybook@gmail.com**

• Show this book to people working with kids, educators and people trying to prevent or heal sexual assault against children. We will work to get them more copies, if they write to **couragepartybook@gmail.com**

If you want to volunteer to get this book out, to help kids have Courage Parties, instead of "conflicting messages," we need advisors, creative thinkers, web wizards, musicians, roller derby skaters, comix fans, big mouths, kind hearts and coronets.

Text   **Call**   **Chat**

YOU DON'T HAVE TO HIDE WHAT HAPPENED

CHILDHELP NATIONAL CHILD ABUSE HOTLINE

1-800-4-A-CHILD

(1-800-422-4453)

www.childhelphotline.org

24/7 | Confidential | We're Here to Help

 **Children's Bureau**   This project is supported by Grant No. 90CA1855 from the Administration on Children, Youth and Families, Children's Bureau US Department of Health and Human Services. 

MICROCOSM · PUBLISHING

Global labor conditions are bad, and our roots in industrial Cleveland in the 70s and 80s made us appreciate the need to treat workers right. Therefore, our books are MADE IN THE USA.

MICROCOSM PUBLISHING is Portland's most diversified publishing house and distributor with a focus on the colorful, authentic, and empowering. Our books and zines have put your power in your hands since 1996, equipping readers to make positive changes in their lives and in the world around them. Microcosm emphasizes skill-building, showing hidden histories, and fostering creativity through challenging conventional publishing wisdom with books and bookettes about DIY skills, food, bicycling, gender, self-care, and social justice. What was once a distro and record label was started by Joe Biel in his bedroom and has become among the oldest independent publishing houses in Portland, OR. We are a politically moderate, centrist publisher in a world that has inched to the right for the past 80 years.

Some adult books about consent from www.Microcosm.Pub

CONSENSUALITY
Navigating Feminism, Gender, and Boundaries Towards Loving Relationships
Rae Allan

SEX FROM SCRATCH
MAKING YOUR OWN RELATIONSHIP RULES
SARAH MIRK

Support
Feminist Relationship Tools to Heal Yourself and End Rape Culture
cindy crabb

LEARNING GOOD CONSENT
Building Ethical Relationships in a Complicated World
cindy crabb

SUBSCRIBE!

For as little as $13/month, you can support a small, independent publisher and get every book that we publish— delivered to your doorstep!

www.Microcosm.Pub/BFF

PESTS UNITE!
MICROCOSM PUBLISHING.COM

More books for empowered adults and teens

"WILL INSPIRE A NEW GENERATION TO FIGHT FOR THEIR FUTURE."
—TOM HAYDEN, ACTIVIST AND AUTHOR
TEENAGE REBELS
SUCCESSFUL HIGH SCHOOL ACTIVISTS FROM THE LITTLE ROCK 9 TO THE CLASS OF TOMORROW
DAWSON BARRETT
FOREWORD BY MARK RUDD OF THE WEATHER UNDERGROUND

IF YOU'RE FREAKING OUT, READ THIS
A COPING WORKBOOK FOR BUILDING GOOD HABITS, BEHAVIORS, AND HOPE FOR THE FUTURE
SIMONE DEANGELIS
AND FAITH G. HARPER, PHD, LPC-S, ACS, ACN
AUTHOR OF UNF-CK YOUR BRAIN

FRIENDING
GINA HANDLEY SCHMITT, MA, LMHC
CREATING MEANINGFUL, LASTING ADULT FRIENDSHIPS

This is Your Brain on
DEPRESSION
Creating Your Path to Getting Better
FAITH G. HARPER, PhD, LPC-S, ACS, ACN
Author of Unf*ck Your Brain

This is Your Brain on
ANXIETY
What Happens and What Helps
FAITH G. HARPER, PhD, LPC-S, ACS, ACN

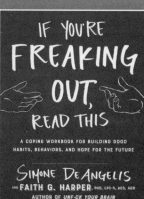

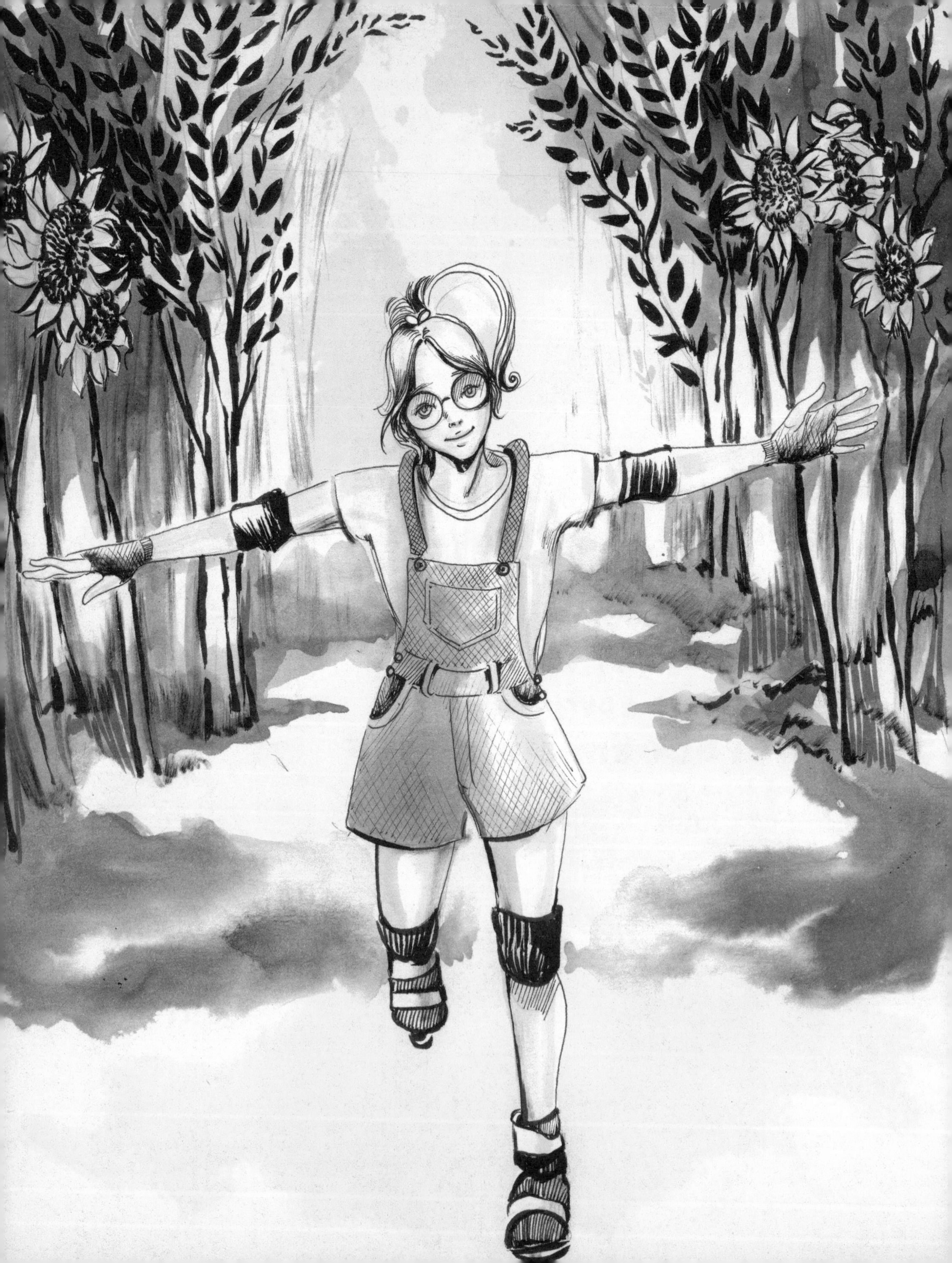

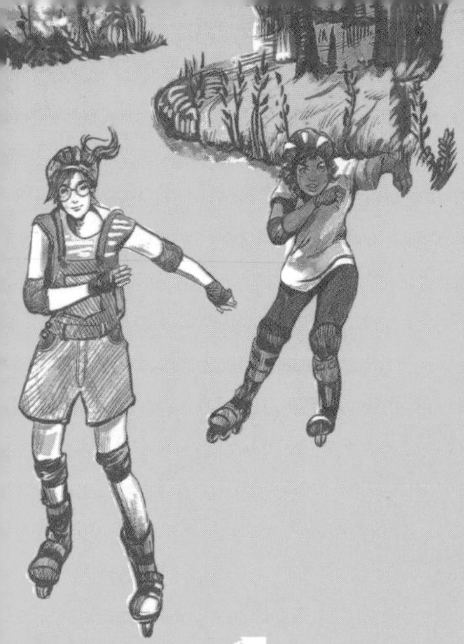
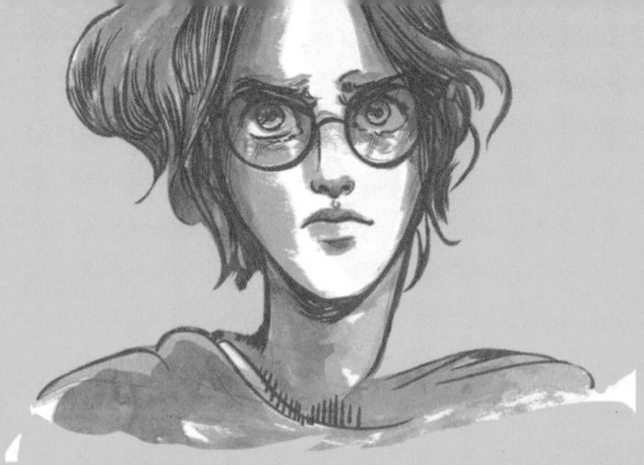
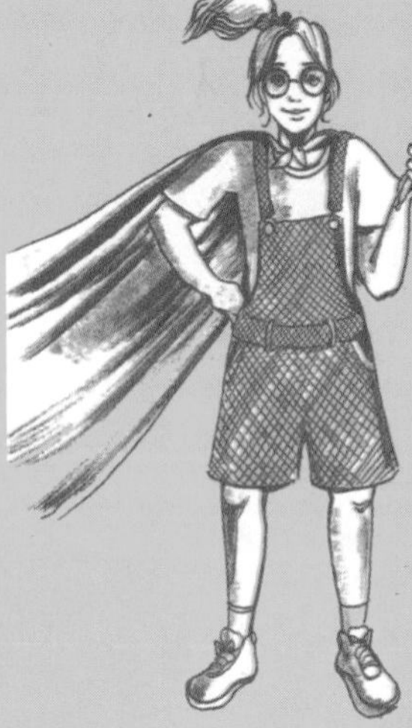
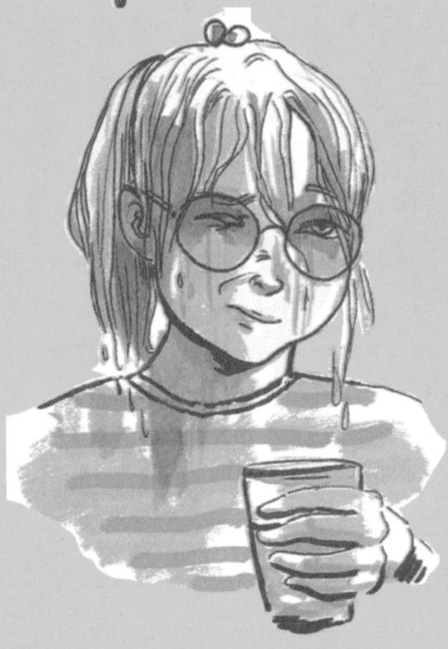
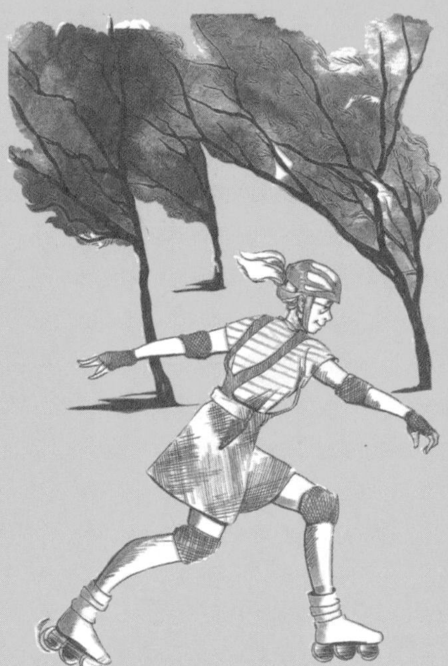
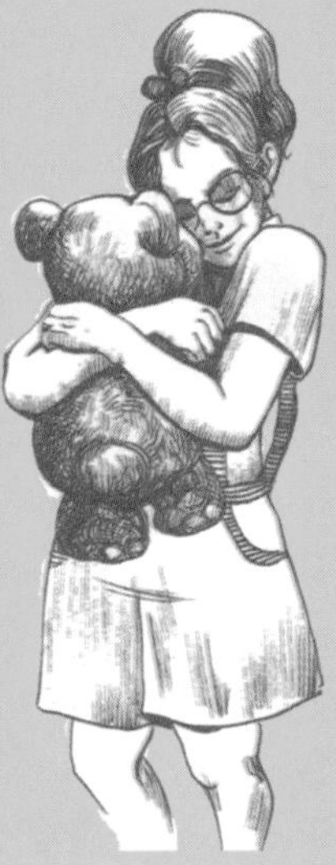
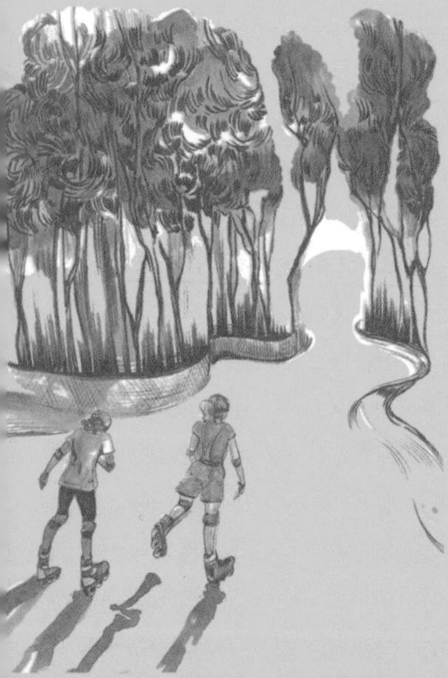
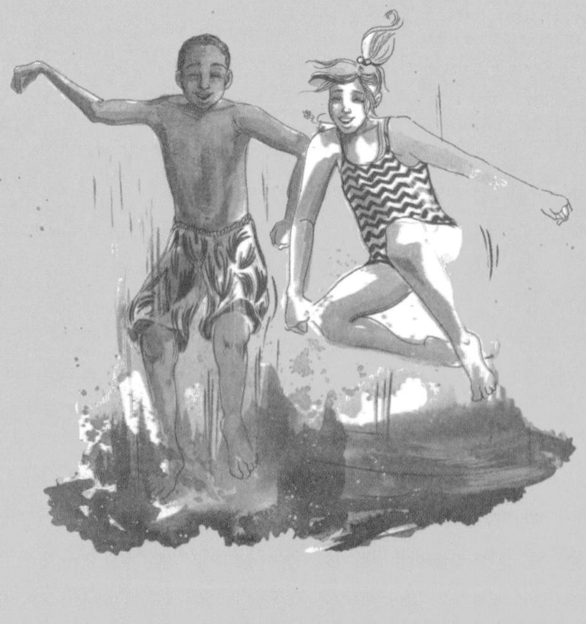
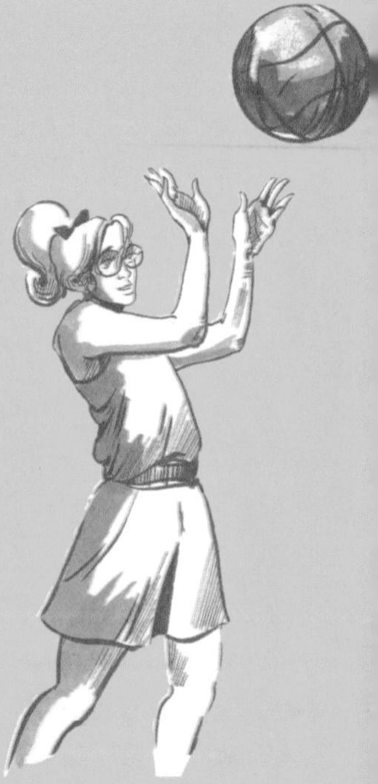